FLYING LESSONS

A journey into self-realization

by Laima Druskis

ACKNOWLEDGEMENTS

I agree with Hillary Clinton, "It takes a village."

First of all I want to thank my parents. They saw something in each other, that we call love. They acted upon it and created a family. I am the oldest of three girls.

Secondly, this book would have never been written without the persistent patience, prodding, and love lavished on me by my teachers that I share in this book: Joseph Rael and Sally Perry, both of them internationally known healers and authors.

Thirdly, this person, Laimute Laima Elena Druskis could not have written this book without the deep spiritual guidance of my Guru: Mahamandaleshwar Yug Purush Swami Paramanand Giriji Maharaj.

It is only in hind sight that I realize my youngest sister, Marquerite and middle sister Lee came into this world to help me mature. As the oldest, I assumed I was helping them. It's as if before they were born we had made a contract to help each other on our paths of self-discovery. Even now, Lee supports me and calls wanting to share "The Daily Word."

Barbara Bryan and I met the first day of college. We hated each other instantly and because of the magnetic system of Karma, became best friends for life. Her family also opened their hearts to me: her father George was the voice of CBS and her mother, Mona a ballerina. These days Barbara can be found at the Interactive Café in Santa Monica. She and I have explored islands together: the British Isles, Santa Cruz Islands, Manhattan, even the islands of our shared psyche. She is the first one I go to for support. "What do you think, will I ever finish this?" Barbara shows no mercy and that's what I often need; the truth and sometimes I listen.

Linda Nathan Marks was the second person in my life who consistently asked me about my writing, year after year. Her parents collected art from the CoBrA movement; her own zest for the arts was something important that we shared. Linda also founded the Crystal Quilt, a feminist organization in New York City, that brought women together to make connections between our personal, political, and spiritual experiences. She has been a supporter of my creative process for more than one lifetime and I am forever grateful.

I could not have gathered my healing tools and began that process without Jane Jennings-Peterson. Jane is an explorer and has no fear of finding the best of the best. Without any hesitation, she would hunt down people that were the laureates of their field: Astrology, BioGeometry, Criminology. Jane would ferret out where they were and then we would go to expand our minds and sail to shores most have never seen.

Every dancer and Chief, who has committed their lives to carrying on the tradition of the Long Dance and the Sun Moon Dance, has given me energy to sit and write. I am thankful and humbled.

Included in this tapestry of Light workers and healers, is the Rael family. Benito, thank you for explaining the intricacies of the dances and Tyo for teaching me to sing to the rocks for the lodge. Without them there would be no grace in my journey.

Writing was easy. The detail work after the manuscript was hard. When you pray for help, good things happen in threes: Ann Evans, John John and John Zulli. Ann shared with me her process as an accomplished writer; John John introduced me to his extraordinary family; maybe it was meeting his mother that gave me the idea for the title of this book. John Zulli helped me to see myself anew.

Evan Clayburg, my graphic designer worked his magic on the computer to create the book jacket and interior design. His easy-going nature allowed me not to panic while looking into the world of fonts and graphic wonderment.

Every damsel in distress needs a knight in shining armor; mine was Chuck Stewart. He is brilliant and his mind only stops when he is on the dance floor. The author of seventeen books and soon to be finished revision of Hamlet, he came to my aid, asking no questions, making no judgment. His emails would arrive with copy cleaned, words of wisdom and then he was gone into the night, no pun intended.

Donna Pizzi, my content editor was suggested by Ann Evans. It wasn't until our third phone conversation that she finally stopped talking for a moment and said, "You really don't know who I am." She was right. "When you were practicing Reiki ten years ago, I was one of your clients." We went on to discuss that extraordinary last Reiki session, in which I played the crystal bowls and she had an amazing experience that would envision her writing a novel, that she is working on now. As my mother would say, "A circle is round." Thank you Donna for helping me weave together the stories of this journey.

My village of helpers are global and some undetected as of yet to my conscious awareness. Thank you.

CONTENTS

CONTENTS

THIS BOOK IS DEDICATED

To all the women and children in
Auschwitz, who stood in line
Frozen with fear.
In a dream not long ago,
I was one of them.

CHAPTER ONE
"Joseph"

Joseph Rael wasn't tall or classically handsome for a Native American. In 1987, we didn't call them Native Americans. He was an Indian. Besides, no one was a native in Brooklyn. Foreign, displaced, lost, but not native. We were all from somewhere else, so how in the world did we know what a native looked like. Maybe that's why I went to see him. Although I can't really remember why I went to see him. Maybe I was bored. Maybe I was looking and didn't even know it. Maybe something inside wasn't asleep, but I didn't know what that was either. Yet somewhere inside, next to my heart, there was something that wouldn't let me forget that day. In that spot, deep inside, it's always yesterday.

Joseph was given the name Beautiful Painted Arrow. His olive eyes penetrated yours like an arrow and they were beautiful. The sound of his voice was pure velvet. When he spoke, his tongue rolled around inside his mouth, caressing each vowel before it was even spoken. His words touched your face like a mother bending over to wipe porridge off the corners of your mouth. When hearing his voice, you were filled, yet always wanting more.

On that day he was giving a lecture in a private home in Park Slope. I've always used the word home, instead of apartment, because I grew up in a house, not a walk-up flat, with the narrow brick hallways you find in Brooklyn. This apartment had a rectangular living room with three tall windows looking out onto a tree-lined street. Joseph's back was to one of the three windows and on this afternoon the sun reflected off his shoulders sharply, creating a glare around him. It was hard to look at him directly. Golden beams of light kept getting into my eyes, causing them to tear up, and for a moment his image parted into a rainbow. With the jerk of my head, he became whole again and I heard a woman in her forties start to introduce him.

"Joseph Rael is an internationally respected shaman and a master story-teller of Pueblo and Ute descent. He was born on the Southern Ute land. It is my pleasure to introduce you to this unique individual." Joseph's eyes twinkled as this sincere academic recited his credentials. As a photographer, I'd caught that twinkle on film before. Capturing the faces of famous politicians, actors and artists was always a challenge. Capturing their eyes is crucial, as eyes are the true signature of any person's soul.

I took a seat in the back of the room and promptly became agitated. I couldn't sit still. Like an endangered feline jaguar that was cornered. I felt caught in the net of his words. The high-pitched sound that came out of his mouth was familiar, like my mother's Estonian tongue. In her language you could determine the intent of a person's words by the pitch. I leapt out of the chair and began to pace the sparsely decorated room which had suddenly been transformed into a cage.

"Maybe if I found a different way of viewing him I'll get out of this discomfort," I hissed to myself. Folding my arms in front of my chest, my body took on the shape of an all-knowing professional photographer. In my head, I was photographing him. He was the one being captured now. It was just a matter of time before I found the right angle. And yet, my skin was cucumber cold and this was the middle of July. As he spoke, I alternated between standing up, putting my left foot on a chair to ground myself and sitting back down again. Everyone hung on each word he spoke. "The nerve," I snorted under my breath.

I became frantic. Didn't they hear it? It wasn't his words, it was the sounds he was making. My whole body began to vibrate to those sounds. My body felt Joseph's ability to use the "tritone paradox" when speaking. It was the capacity to tone two separate notes an octave apart. One high and one low. Sounding in perfect unison the two tones may be perceived as one. The second tone is a "tritone" – a note exactly halfway between the two octaves. Some people can hear the higher octave. My body was responding to the higher octave without my consent. His truth was known to my body, yet not to me. Something wasn't right with this picture, even a Nikon couldn't help but put this into some frame of logical context for me.

My visual world was being shattered. Something about the light and the sounds coming out of his mouth caused my body to undergo another perceptual shift. He wasn't giving a lecture or prepared speech. He was speaking to the collective consciousness of the group. Somehow, I knew that he knew what everybody was thinking. He spoke to just that. The collective yearning.

I remember him saying, "Sometimes I can see thoughts manifesting as if they were lights. I see thoughts travel across a room in little blocks of light about half an inch long and a quarter of an inch wide. There are spaces in between those little blocks of light. These spaces are thoughts willing to open and ready to manifest new form, even as it's going along. That's how quickly change can occur. Even as we are thinking something out, as it is traveling 20 feet across a room, it can change."

He spoke to our collective yearning and I hated him for touching my heart in that way. I became furious with him. How dare he? How could he? What could I do?

What else, but become his student.

CHAPTER TWO

"Dreaming of the Future in Present Time"

Joseph traveled from New Jersey to Manhattan to teach his fledgling group of followers. Once every six weeks we met in a walk-u just below 14th Street. It was just like every other fourth floor walk-up. This one was filled with cats, overstuffed chairs, and a couch retrieved from Alphabet Land. God knows how they got it up the stairs. In the middle of the room was a barber's chair and that was his emeritus' seat of honor. We gathered to hear his wisdom. His lectures were very free-form. Or so I thought at the time. He felt we would get the information whether we were sitting up taking notes or lying down asleep. I was usually asleep.

Too much, too fast, it wasn't my style.

One evening Joseph addressed the topic of sound. When he was eight years old, he had the task of learning three languages simultaneously; Spanish, English and Tiwa. Until then, he had spoken only Tiwa, his mother's tongue. When Joseph was six, he started his training with his grandfather and four other elders. His grandfather would take him to the underground ceremonial chamber called a Kiva. There he would teach Joseph the vowel sounds and help him see the vibration principles encoded in the human gene pool. Joseph began to understand the symbolic power of the vowel sounds. Over and over, he would repeat the vowel sounds: A for purification, E for placement, I for awareness, O for childlike innocence and U for carrying. By chanting the vowel sounds in a word, he discovered the principal meaning of a word. For example, chanting the word table, the vowels "a" and "e" were present. From this, Joseph felt that the table was like a flat plane, which allowed for purity of placement to be understood. Joseph was like E. F. Hutton to me. When he spoke I listened. Somehow my higher self knew there were great dividends to be had in his thoughts.

One afternoon, while Joseph was talking, I fell asleep. In my mind's eye were pictures of the Bishop of Canterbury sweeping his hand across a table, admonishing a little Indian boy for thinking the earth was round. That was Joseph, thinking outside the box. For Joseph, language was an extension of the earth. The earth was the symbol of our vast self. The consciousness that expressed itself in movement, constantly changing. That was the heart of Mother Earth. Like our body, the earth has different parts and so language evolved from its placement on the earth. People spoke of this consciousness in the forms of different languages. Animals were different in each part of the earth and they reflected that differentiation of consciousness. Everything on earth, all that sits on the surface, is part of the creation story of consciousness.

Waking up, I began to understand how he spoke to the group consciousness in Brooklyn when I first met him and he touched our collective awareness. I realized now, the English language was not a barrier, it didn't matter if some of his students were from South America, Lithuania or upstate New York. We were learning universal concepts, language was the vehicle that concepts traveled on and our breath pulled it into our being. The Tiwa language taught him that life was a metaphor. For Joseph, everything was made up of principal ideas that were carried in sound. When Joseph introduced new ideas, he would speak very slowly and deliberately. While listening to him, I found myself matching his breath. In this way my inner thoughts collapsed and space was available for new ideas to come in.

Like snail mail my thought process crawled in this way: the first, principal ideas were held in words. These universal principals were found by sounding the vowels in each word and the meaning of the vowels gave a broader-vibrational meaning to the specific word.

To me, it was logical that if words held universal principles, there would be no need for questions. The ability to speak a word revealed the meaning inside the spoken word. It was obvious to my mind that if human beings could formulate a question, they knew the answer. Within the words of a question lies the answer.

Again I closed my eyes. Hearing my breath, my thoughts took a left-hand turn toward bliss. I thought to myself, "How lucky am I, to be sitting in this over-stuffed, putrid green cat-hair-filled recliner. What a surprise to come early tonight and snag this position before anyone else. "Front row seat, Druskis." I was ready for direct transmission. "We have lift off, Houston." My lips curled upward into a smile, and my brain danced with ideas of how words held principle ideas. "Words, words, words the bird. Birds the word." That left-hand turn into my brain had taken me into my audio library and I had somehow stepped onto a broken record playing, "Words, words, words the bird." A vision of big yellow bird from Sesame Street appeared inside me.

As if picking up a cue from a movie script, Joseph got up and walked to the table with the sleepy orange tabby on it. I had taken a liking to this tabby and named him Schrodinger. With the index finger of his right hand, Joseph pointed to him. Instantly Schrodinger woke up, his body frozen in space, realizing he might be part of a shamanic experiment in the materialization of a physical form through sound. I woke feeling Schrodinger's stress.

My eyes widened; surely Schrodinger was right. Joseph, however, was of no mind and continued his discourse, "Everything that is said conveys a metaphoric sense of life, of time, of space. Everything is made up of the principal ideas and for each idea there is a sound. In Tiwa, "Poh" means "blowing breath," and it also stands for vibration. Sound is made of vibration. For a longtime the focus of my life was to understand all physical forms as sound and vibration of the infinite self, and how to become a working listener to those forms."

Joseph stroked the cat with the palm of his right hand and made the sound, "aaa." He looked at us, as if we should understand the principle meaning of c-A-t. Schrodinger arched his back and hissed the vowel "a." I was sure of that.

"Everything is encoded in the gene pool. Whatever language we speak, we are speaking from that culture. Beneath that there is a code that can be understood universally. To become conscious of all that, we have ceremony." Schrodinger jumped off the table as if Joseph's last sentence had shoved him to the very edge of a new reality. With electrified orange hair, Schrodinger scampered into the bathroom to hide. My attention was peaked. I was right, Schrodinger was going to be used for a scientific ceremony.

Poor Schrodinger.

Joseph glanced at the bathroom door and continued, "I love ceremony. It is a way to conceptualize the process of metaphor. Everything that exists. Everything. Every object, every action, every experience is actualizing principal ideas. When we dance the bear dance or the corn dance, it is our way of expressing devotion for the Holiest of all Holies. For me, dancing is like going to church. My whole body is in prayer when I am dancing. When something comes up for me and I need an answer, I just dance. We dance to expand and therefore expand our awareness."

Suddenly, I became aware of my body becoming relaxed. As he was talking about dancing, my body melted, responding to his words and images. My shoulders dropped and I pushed myself further into the cat-hair couch. This position created pressure on my joints and opened my knees and elbows. I could feel the movement of energy squeezing out from my torso to my extremities and back again. This back-and-forth flow of energy created a type of internal pressure. Not an anxious pressure. I imagined my body like a Ferrari getting an oil change. Joseph's voice faded, and my attention was drawn to my mouth. It was dry. My tongue kept rotating, keeping the cavity moist. My tongue reached up and stroked the roof of my mouth again and again. It was a sensuous movement, relaxing me even more and connecting me with the future vision of Joseph's first drum dance in dream time. Now my whole attention was on the first drum dance. In this dream state – inside my head, I drove a red Ferrari – I journeyed back to the beginning of the first dance.

Joseph had invited us all to the four corners, at the Ute reservation. On that sacred land is where the first drum dance took place in the summer of 1987. That same dryness was in my mouth now, as the door of the Delta 647 opened and a blanket of scorching air engulfed me. This airport reminded me of the one in Indianapolis, where I grew up. In my child's mind, I remembered waving goodbye to my father as he went on one of his monthly business trips.

Now in this dream, the Durango airport had the same short runways. Young men pushing handcarts every which way and delivering baggage to oblong Quonset huts, while wandering families found each other off the runway. A bitter taste of anxiety filled my mouth, as questions rose up in my mind: who would pick me up? Was there a Time Zone change? Bile kept pushing up in my throat as each new question formulated inside my brain. The flyer for Joseph's dance read, "Bring tent, buckets to store water, food and all camping equipment." There was a telephone number listed. "Thank God!" I thought to myself, "A connection to civilization. There is a way out."

Whenever I participate in a spiritual activity, I suspend my normal headset of expectations. I tried to do it this time. The reason for this behavior was to help the mind become nonjudgmental. With internal expectations, one cannot stay in present time. There is a jumping back and forth between internal needs and external reality.

Still the questions. Who would pick me up? Maybe I'll have to go to the dance site alone, but where is it? Where does the Ute tribe begin? Sure, at one time the whole territory belonged to them, but what about now?

Lost inside my head, I walked right past a young man holding a cardboard sign that read: "Joseph's Workshop."

The young man politely touched my shoulder and asked, "Are you here for the drum dance?" His voice had a comforting Rio cadence. Actually, any cadence was comforting as long as someone was going to answer my questions. "My name is Buck. Are you here for Joseph's workshop?"

"There!" I said to myself, "You see…each moment will unfold into the trusting arms of the next. Trust! Trust Druskis!"

"Yes." I blurted out. I inhaled as much oxygen as my lungs could hold and moments later, remembered to let it out. "Yes, that's me," I said.

Suddenly, a huge knot started to build in the back of my neck. It felt like the end of a giant fist was pushing up my spine, its knuckles cramming pain into every part of my brain. What a headache. The altitude. I was experiencing the kind of pounding only a migraine headache could produce.

"Concentrate on what he is saying. That will take your focus off the pain and smile. Give them that Delta Zeta smile, Druskis."

Something inside was trying to comfort me. But my facial muscles were directly connected to the pounding and I couldn't smile. Buck was the spitting image of a Marlboro man. A dusty light blue cotton shirt and tight Levi's accentuated his lean, tan body. His ruffled blonde hair fit under a legendary pale gray Stetson. A four-beaver pelt Stetson could keep your head dry from the worst summer storms and a lifetime of sweat. His indigo eyes took in everything. He glanced back and forth from me to the cart where three navy duffle bags were stacked.

Joseph had talked about not eating or drinking for three days of the dance. This process would clean the body and our senses would become very sharp. If we were aware and conscious, each dancer could learn more about themselves and expand their reality of who they were.

This method was all good a well, but my fear demanded a back up system. My dark blue duffel bags were filled with "just-in-case" necessities: a one-year supply of soy milk, honey bars, "quick" energy vitamins, salt tablets, candles, cooking utensils and chewing gum. The other two marine green bags contained clothing, shoes and jewelry that came under the heading: things to wear while drum dancing. Check the summer issue of Vogue, that was my inspiration. With all that loaded in the truck, I climbed into the backseat and there was my first encounter with Sally Perry. "Dear God," I mused to myself, "She looks like a lost housewife from Connecticut." Her hair was piled high upon her head. The mass was held together by bobby pins and a quart of hairspray. Her eye make-up rivaled Tammy Baker. Certainly, she had just stepped out of the cosmic shopping mall. I sized her up real fast, no connection here. Yet her eyes and Mona Lisa knowing smile were very disconcerting.

"What's the trouble?" Sally asked with a Southern accent.

"I have a terrible headache. It's got to be the altitude. I have aspirin somewhere." I turned to look inside my backpack.

"Here. Let me fix it. I'm a healer." Sally placed her left hand over my heart and her right hand on the back of my neck.
The dulling pain and headache were instantly gone.

In the outside world, everything is easily defined. All the rules are set. Doctors wear white coats and synthetic medicine is needed to recover from the slightest discomfort.

"There. Do you feel better? I live in Virginia Beach and I've been involved with the Edgar Casey Foundation. You've heard of them? I have this lovely beauty shop in a hotel near there. Very convenient. Buck, do you need money for gas?" Sally batted her eyelashes at him.

We both gave five dollars and the truck lurched forward creating a dust storm across the most beautiful country I had ever seen. All my childhood Sky King dreams kept flying in front of me on route 45.

CHAPTER THREE

"The First Dance is the Best Dance"

After checking in with Joseph, the second order of business was to find a campsite. This was a daunting activity that was making me very nervous. The third order of business was to ask for help. We were standing in a grove of pines and shrub, not far from the parking area, where we were dropped off.

"Buck, do you think…" I cleared my throat and started again, "Buck, do you mind helping me find a campsite and tell me why you figure it's a good one." My immigrant insecurities were rising up to face me. Placement, it was all about placaement. Where do I live? What does home feel like?

Buck found a level area under three young pine trees. "If it rains, the pines will break the wind." He started to walk away, then turned on his heels and with half a smile said, "But you'd better make peace with those ants over there."

Not more than 30 feet away was a huge anthill. Quickly, I decided to stay elsewhere. I hadn't forgotten about last year when visiting Joseph on the East Coast. He had asked me to give thanks to the ants by putting corn meal inside their home.
Universally, ants symbolize work, thrift and forethought.

God knows why, but I didn't do the ceremony. Once again it was that tug with male authority. Now I had the opportunity to finish that ceremony, but I didn't have any corn meal. Looking back toward Buck, I mirrored his half-smile, made a left hand turn and headed in the opposite direction to find my own way. As I started walking down a trail, a bumble bee appeared. My father came to mind. The sight of the bee brought me to our backyard in Indianapolis. Father had bought three bee hives. He said there was one hive for each of his girls. At his funeral, while the preacher was holding forth with some forgettable litany, all eyes were riveted to a small swarm of bees trying to get into my father's coffin. It was mesmerizing. The last goodbye to an old friend. I will never forget that moment.

I followed the bumble bee eastward in search of the perfect campsite. It led me to a huge, three-story high cedar tree that reminded me of the Mikmaq warrior who was frightened of dying. Glooskap, his God, turned him into a Cedar tree. The Cedar is a symbol of the Grandmother who can withstand the buffeting of life and live longer than any man. Glooskap told Mikmaq, "I will give you the gift of being a Cedar tree, with the ability to think like a human and reflect upon things. You will have centuries to look upon this situation called death from every conceivable angle." Remembering Glooskap, I knew this was the place.

To the left of the cedar tree was a meandering cattle trail, dotted with deer tracks. On the right, the land gracefully dipped into a five-hundred-foot meadow, with its edge opening onto a rocky riverbed. Here was my home. I wanted to take a picture, but I had intentionally left my camera equipment in California. I was here to experience, not capture a Kodak moment. Too often, I let film replace direct experience.

Sun bleached deer bones were strewn everywhere. They would be my symbolic guide to accomplishing three goals at this dance: First, to open my heart to my body and other people. Secondly, to heal a left and right brain dilemma called dyslexia. Thirdly, to recognize that the gift to make quantum jumps mentally was a double-edged sword. For me, the Big picture was easy; practical small steps were hard to accomplish. The dance would teach me how to take some of those baby steps.

As the sun drifted west, I set up camp. I had made sure to bring a tent that slept at least three. Claustrophobia and anxiety were kissing cousins in my world. There was a need to roll around during sleep. Within three hours, there was perfection inside my tent. It was my home. Next to my sleeping bag, were my survival needs: the gum, soy milk, energy bars and three bags of peanuts from the flight. Cooing to myself, I whispered, "Look, but don't touch." Then I stroked the energy bar box.

It came like a thunder clap. Four of them. The call of the drum. A huge buffalo hide drum, manned by four drummers announcing the beginning of the dance. No one could escape the sound. Everyone headed toward the open dance arena. As the sun set, in what photographers call "sweet light," Joseph gave us instruction on how to dance. The two male leaders shook their rattles and we danced to the middle of the arena where two poles were strung with sage hoops. At the center, we formed two lines and started to shuffle toward a round house, which was to the left of the dance floor. I say "shuffle" because that is what I did, shuffle. "Shuffle on down to Buffalo," I said to myself. "Keep it light. Shuffle on down." Joseph's voice startled the frightened child inside me.

"To create energy, start on your right foot. To resolve conflict, start on your left." Joseph said.

I was having trouble with both feet. I needed energy, so I started with my right foot. Then Joseph had added a hop to our dance step. One, two, three, hop. Simple choreography was baffling me. Energy was draining from my body and from the pores in the bottom of my feet. We hadn't been dancing for more than fifteen minutes. I kept bumping into the next person. "Poor Joseph." I thought to myself, "we are not the spiritual chorus line he had envisioned."

Following the beat of the enormous drum, our two lines of dancers converged, and we moved reluctantly toward the round house. It was two stories high and the roof was covered with freshly cut cedar. Thirty to fifty people could have easily fit inside the structure. We formed a circle, with our hands down by our sides. The drum stopped.

Standing in the center of our circle, Joseph began to describe a three-tiered mental system that each human has. The first level is filled with our everyday thoughts. The second was our value system and deeply ingrained in our psyche. The third tier held our core beliefs. This mental system, he said, guides and colors all information brought into our being.

"During this dance you will begin to discover this system. Pay attention. Be awake."

After he spoke, a stillness permeated the air. With my eyes moving slowly, I watched the 5 o'clock shadow climb the wall and rest on a framed picture of an American eagle. "What were my core beliefs?" I asked in a whisper to the evening night.

Joseph raised his arm, with his right hand he traced the letter "E" on a canvas in the air. "Let's chant the letter 'E'."

We sounded flat as a group. Our voices strained to find a level pitch. While we were chanting, he divided us into two groups. The first group stopped chanting. He pointed to a wooden ladder that leaned against a hole in the roof. Each person started to climb up. When it was my turn, I wasn't afraid of the height, which was abnormal for me. I kept repeating the mantra, "These are strong hands." Indeed, they were. Stepping onto the roof, I felt like a star. The chanting came through the roof and tickled my feet. In a little girl's voice, I whispered "I'm home." In my heart I knew I had come from a dwarf planet which hadn't been discovered yet. In the year 2003, the scientific community would discover Eris. Then it was titled: UB313; the largest dwarf planet to be seen. It was seventy billion miles from the sun and took five hundred and sixty years to orbit it. "I can see you." The wind carried my thoughts to the sage grove below and into the heavens.

After climbing down the stairs, something fundamentally had changed inside of me. Some sort of newness had entered my body. Planting my feet firmly on the ground, I began to chant the vowel "E". Before a second breath filled my lungs, one of the dancers staggered, coughed, falling forward right onto his face. Everyone watched in silence, as he staggered to his feet. He seemed startled, as if awakened from a dream. Smiling, he spread his arms out to make wings and promptly fell backward with a thud, causing sheets of dust to cover him. His body was a crumbled heap. "Some being has discarded his body right there in front of me. We need help. Right here in River City. Help!" I screamed inside. "What should I do?" Every cell in my body began to panic.

My mouth became sandpaper dry, not a sound came out, as the acid thought came into my throat, "Who can chant when they're beginning to drop like flies?" "It's time to go home, right!" My pupils were large and crow black. I was looking at my greatest fear right in front of me. Falling on my face and passing out or falling backwards and hitting my head. Death with a thud.

We were all startled by the dancer's fall. Our collective gasp circled the room, before passing over and then falling on top of him. The sound of our disbelief smothered him with shame. Quickly another dancer bent over, shook him and helped him up. The fallen dancer swayed as he rose. A child-like smile formed once more upon his face.

"Dear God, this fucker is supposed to be a lead dancer," I thought. "Great. And he's the first to fall!"

Anger mixed with terror filled my stomach. I couldn't concentrate. This was not my image of a lead male dancer. Who can chant after witnessing that? As long as I kept my external excuses intact, the fear inside seemed to be in check. Kodak pictures inside my head began to shift to the first time I was in a sweat lodge with Joseph. A woman jumped up and crawled out of the lodge after the first round. She clearly felt claustrophobic. Gasping for air and space, she leapt like a frog. One, two, and she was gone. After she left, Joseph thanked her for that action. She had embodied our collective fear and taken it out of the lodge.

Remembering that time in the lodge, I thought to myself, "What a brave and sensitive guy." My ever-present critic jumped at the chance to admonish me for not being as sensitive. "You, Lithuanian oaf! You feel nothing! Nothing at all."

I closed my eyes in shame and began to listen to the night instead of my thoughts. My voice dropped an octave and the sound of "E" pushed itself into the round house. We chanted the sound for the longest while. Time seemed to wander in and out of everyone's awareness. It rose through the hole in the roof sailing into a midnight lapis sky.

Outside, we danced on into darkness, trying to remember how or why we had begun. Our shadows crisscrossed between three huge bonfires that gave us light to see. Feet were going every which way. Three steps and a hop. Maybe two steps and a hop, stop. Bumping and stumbling. Dust rising, security falling. We were beating everything familiar into the clay. My body was losing ground. Somewhere I was floating inside. Joseph raised his arm and we collided into one another. He asked us to stay silent.

"Do not share your experience. Nurture it in silence. Let it seed. Let it grow inside you."

As we headed toward our tents, flashlights lit the night sky like fireflies. With that thought, I remembered I had forgotten mine. There was plenty of moonlight, but could the pictures in my memory match what was out there? I started using tents to navigate.

"Make a left at Cathy's green army tent. Bob's sleeping bag is over to the right. Ah, yesss," I hissed. "This is the Douglas fir. I remember it." As I slithered along, speaking softly to myself with a forked tongue. The realization came to me that I had chosen my campsite furthest from civilization. By day, it seemed reasonable, even poetic. By night without a flashlight, it was disastrous. "Damn the night." The words created the blackest hole I had ever known inside me.

"I should be like Rodgers and Hammerstein. 'The King and I,' yes? I whistle a happy tune. Is this not Siam?" I tried to smile and forget that

Joseph told us to be silent. I needed to find happy. I needed a happy tune. My lips puckered, air came out but no sound. I listened to myself trying to be brave. Lips puckered, with no sound.

"Be here now, Ram Dass." But this "now" had changed too much for me to feel safe. I was so frightened, I had lost "sight" of what was in front of me.

I thought of Byron Smith, the reporter I worked with while at Indiana University News Bureau. We were an amazing team, I did the photography and he interviewed the people I photographed. The news bureau would send out pictures and an audio clip. The pictures would go to the wire services and Byron's audio clips would go to local and national radio stations. He had an amazing sense of where everything was. Byron had pictures of the whole campus in his head. Being blind, Byron's internal vision was keenly developed and we needed that.

On the way to assignments, I would get us lost driving on campus. I had little sense of direction. Street names or addresses never stuck in my head. Byron would get us back on track. "Okay, tell me what's on the corner and I'll tell you where to go. Let's not be late. And, Druskis, we cannot park in that lot ahead. If you do," he would say, his words admonishing me for the four hundredth time, "you are going to get another ticket. How many is that this month, Druskis?" He never called me by my first name and he never got us lost. If I listened to his directions, we always got there on time. It never felt odd to me that I had no internal visual sense as a photographer and this blind man standing next to me, had excellent internal visual acuity. We were a perfect couple.

For the first time in my life, I asked the question: "How did he do that inner vision stuff?"

Now panic spread like cancerous cells. I was lost. I kept holding my breath. I couldn't see inside or out. "Concentrate only on walking." Joseph would say, "Wa, ma, chi." It became my mantra as I stepped slowly from one black space into the next. I stopped and closed my eyes. When I opened them, my visual awareness was enhanced. Shadows stood out and moonlight came streaming down between the branches of cedar trees in the grove next to me.

One of the most profound learning experiences of this dance was beginning to crystallize. If I focused on what I was supposed to be doing NOW, all of my emotions would dissolve and a timeless fascination with experiencing the present moment would take over. Boundless energy would surge through my body. I experienced this while dancing, awakening, brushing my teeth; the most mundane tasks became exciting and energizing. One foot in front of the other. One step at a time. Right, left. Right, left.

Then he appeared. Not a sound was made. Moon glitter caught my eye and I cupped my hand in front of my right eye to focus. Was this really happening?

The most magnificent owl I had ever seen stood in front of me. There are seventeen species of owls in North America and this majestic Great Gray Owl was easily five feet tall. I gasped at his height. He turned his head left than right to see, rather than moving his eyes. These owls have specialized feathers which enable them to fly within inches from their prey without being detected. His wing span was wider than I was tall, or so it seemed. The owl's wings have feathers covered with small hooks and bows, that would break up the flowing air into smaller, micro-turbulence. The smaller the turbulence, the less sound. His velvety down feathers on his legs would absorb any remaining noise he would make. He was the silent night eagle. He waited for me to stop shaking. A nervous "whoooo" came out of my mouth and "Why!" The Great Gray Owl had flown from the direction of the north to the South. He looked at me as if I were a juvenile trying to impress an elder. While staring into his eyes, the realization came that he was a human, dreaming. He had transported his consciousness into this time zone as a Great Gray Owl. I cocked my head to look closer and confirm my suspicions. Those were human eyes and he was a master healer in the form of an owl. He had flown from the wisdom of the North into the emotions of the South, where I was.

I took one micro-step forward. As I leaned even closer to get a better look at him, he winked at me.

Quickly, all the superstitions about owls started attacking me. "Someone died. Maybe it's going to be you. What does he want? What am I supposed to do? Forget it! Shut up." I begged myself to calm down and become rational. This was a time for formal introduction to the world's largest species of owls. I felt awkward and unworthy. Somewhere inside of me I wanted to cry with joy. Slowly I removed my gray felt hat and reverently said stretching out the "how" in how do you do? "We haven't been introduced before."

He swiveled his head slightly to the right. Keeping his laser eyes on me as if I might have been a rat, he was going to pounce on in the next moment. Then he up and flew away.

Arriving back at my tent, the loveliest mother owl began singing a lullaby to her children in the cedar tree above. As I zipped up my forest green sleeping bag, the lullaby carried me into the deepest sleep.

Awaking next morning, I remembered saying to myself, "I would have died if he had spoken in English, let alone Lithuanian." That's why I always tried to speak to animals first. I was scared that they might speak to me. So, I always started the conversation. You can't listen while talking. If the owl spoke, it would have dissolved all my known sense of what is real. My everyday world would have crumbled in front of me and that had already happened with Joseph in Manhattan.

I remembered it like yesterday. It was during a healing session in lower Manhattan, Joseph dissolved in front of me. I looked around the room, under the rug, behind me. Every hair on my body stood at attention, every cell cried in disbelief. My heart started pounding, quicker and quicker. He was gone. He had disappeared. Nothing.

Now I realized it must have been some sort of test and I failed. Like most people, I worked hard at keeping my reality intact. It's not fair when you slip so easily into other realms, while your body and senses aren't prepared.

Instantly he reappeared. "It's ok. You get scared too easily."

That was true.

That first night of the dance I slept deeply, covered in a gray blanket of unconsciousness. No dreams. No memories. No fear.

CHAPTER FOUR

"The First Day"

This first day's attire was a cotton night shift, fluffy pink gym socks and Reeboks. My nose was caked with number 50 sun block. Lips were sealed with pure petroleum jelly. In keeping with the American theme, a red, white and blue bandana kept my smelly hair out of my greasy face.

There was very little morning light and there was chill in the air. "What the hell," I mused, "I feel like a classic beauty. It's a good day to dance your heart out."

When I reached the dance site, most of the others were milling about, deciding where they were going to dance. Somehow, facing west seemed right to me. This direction represented the physical realm. On each side of the poles was a walkway made of rock circles. The middle of each circle was filled with Cedar bark. The bark felt like sponge when standing on it. In the middle were four poles holding up rope with Sage hoops hanging from it.

When we found our places Joseph gave us some rules. "First, try the one, two, three, hop step. Second, if you want to rest, leave the dance arena. No talking. When you want to move to the other side of the dance floor, step out of your circle and dance to the center, wait by the Sage hoops for a moment, and then pass between them and dance toward an empty Cedar Circle. Never dance in front of your fellow dancers. When you reach your Cedar Circle, decide what foot to start on and then step into the circle to dance. Do not concentrate on anything special, allow your eyes to pass along the sage hoops. If you have a vision, or encounter a being, stay grounded and keep dancing. If some new reality opens up inside the hoops, hold it for a moment and then shift your eyes to the next hoop. Allow your vision to scan from left to right. Remember yesterday, I had asked you to find a cedar stick? The stick you carved from Cedar, you should keep. Do not lose it. Feel the bark, make the wood part of you. The tree represents greatness. Dance on the skin of these trees, feel the greatness in you and the trees."

Joseph then showed us a dance step. Right foot step, left foot step, hop. One, two, hop gets boring very fast. But the chatter in my head was worse. It felt like the Nuremberg Trial was being re-broadcast inside me and I was playing every part.

When the body begins to break down, so does the genetic psyche. I felt as though I was locked inside a phone booth while listening to ugly conversations I didn't want to hear. After berating everyone here, I started on myself. "You can't do the step right. Does this have any meaning? Will you ever change? You spent all this money to get here. Not a penny saved. You're falling apart." I started to cry huge baby tears. I was ashamed and lost. I was looking at myself and I didn't like the person who was appearing, worse still, there was no compassion to be found anywhere.

"Focus on what you are supposed to be doing now," I told myself. One, two, three and my mind leapt to the realization that dancing was the only thing to do. Wiping tears away with my forearm, a vision of myself sitting in the Zendo in upstate New York appeared. The words of John Daido Loori, the Zen Master of the monastery lifted me up, "If the left arm is burned, does not the right hand automatically move to protect it? The mind does not think I have burned myself. Maybe my right hand will consider helping the left one out of the flames. The left and right are connected by the body. We are connected through invisible ways you do not yet understand," said John.

For a moment, everyone seemed to be a reflection of my internal state.

The man across from me was perfectly in step. "He's dancing very well. You're fine, Druskis." Another dancer fell and pounded her frustrations into the ground with her sticks. I smiled, "That's me." A golden wave of compassion washed over me, the likes of which I had not felt since a child on

Riverside Drive, petting the family Afghan named Pluto. The gold circled my body and washed away the self-absorbed muck around my shoulders. "I don't have to save my father. Be anyone. For anyone. Just dance."

The warm light was healing. Rods of trusting energy began to penetrate every pore. John's voice came back to me, "After going up the mountain, then you must come down. You must not stay. It is our way to return."

"Hamburgers. One, two, three hamburgers." The hungry mind had returned, landing directly in the stomach. "Hamburgers! Give me a Big Mac. Can you taste it yet, Druskis?"

One, two, three, hop, my feet did not listen. One, two, three, hop.

It was mid-morning and the sun was beating down on us in full force. Joseph waved his hands. The drummers stopped. Break time. Each of us scattered to find shade under the surrounding Cedar trees. The soil was baked russet and the summer drought had dried the grass, stunting the growth of the sage bushes. Red ants were everywhere, the land was theirs. They would attack any human sitting on it.

For Joseph, the ant symbolized the ability to work as a group. The Chinese call them the "righteous insect." The ant is orderly and knows how to follow the command of its leader. In the Hindi and Persian mythology, huge ants would guard treasures. Some cultures gave them the magical attributes: patience, stamina and the ability to plan for the future.

I sat on the earth next to a colony and watched them do what I could not: have patience so that I might plan for a future.

My sense of smell had begun to return that morning. I had lost most of that ability working in a unventilated photographic lab. I delighted in smelling the world again. When I had moved to the west coast, doing sweat lodges had cleaned my liver, opened my nostrils and saved my life. Now not eating for several days, my body had detoxed enough to open up my sense of smell even wider to the sage growing everywhere. Sage, is the flower of immortality that possesses medical gifts to heal the body. The Romans considered Sage sacred. Christ spoke of it so highly that harvesting its leaves became an important ceremony. Gathering the leaves from a sage bush, was no ordinary gardening activity. Roman servants wore white while gathering the sage leaves using special bronze and silver tools.

The smell of sage reminded me of attending a lodge in which the floor was covered with freshly picked sage. Very quickly the lodge filled with its aroma and the smell flooded my chest, with its antiseptic and antibacterial properties. I began to cough, as if my lungs were being stung by a hundred bees. I tried to listen as the sweat lodge leader told us about its healing properties: tonic for the female reproductive tract; helping with digestion; calming the nerves and clearing emotional obstructions from the mind, promoting clarity. The clarity for me was addressing the many family addictions. Coughing, slowly I began to see one of mine. This was the addiction of seeing of body as "me". I was more than my body and I was discovering this at the dance.

The dance was set for three days, one of the most important moments of the dance came at the end of the first day. Facing west, I developed an awareness of becoming a witness to my own body. I watched myself dancing in slow motion. A being of brilliant light came toward me, I raised my right hand to accept its outstretched radiance. We touched and the light went through me and became part of me. At that moment, consciousness merged with the witness and a transformational shift was felt inside. I heard Joseph's voice in the background, "Let the being go through you slowly." My eyes opened wider, as I realized I was watching a slow-motion movie. The movie of the dance was being observed frame-by-frame. Am I asleep? Am I dreaming? Am I awake? I am somehow losing my mind, yet I am still here. Who is watching this movie?"

The movie ended, stepping outside the Cedar Circle I caught my balance. It was as if I came to my normal senses. Hysterical laughter bubbled up into froth, as "I came to my senses." I was frightened of losing my mind. My father did. For moments, my sister did, too. Now me? Then I walked back a few paces, knelt down and started crying. Placing my head on the ground cleared the mind and centered the body. I wiped my eyes with my bandanna, got up and started dancing again. I used this process of grounding several times throughout the dance to integrate the light.

During the afternoon break, I laid down under some Juniper trees. Looking up at the sky through the green branches, I saw and heard an eagle fly. Whoosh. The air was so clean and our bodies so refined, I could listen to the eagle fly. The eagle circled the corner of my left eye as he surveyed the dance site. He lifted the air with his wings. I wondered if there wasn't some aerodynamic connection between flight and dancing.

During this break from the dance, I decided to lay a trail to my tent so the trip at night would not have any glitches. I was fearful of getting lost or meeting the owl again. My eyes moved quickly down the hill, past the trailers, parked cars, and three haggard Sage bushes. What would I use to mark the trail? What would catch the reflection of my flashlight? My memory raced back to being a teenager in the Lithuanian Scouts, on the shore of Lake Michigan. One of the tests given to us was finding our way back to camp by moonlight. We were blindfolded, and each girl had a partner. Our left hands were tied together. I can remember sitting in the back of the Jeep, bumping along feeling frightened, with a mixture of excitement. All of our senses were heightened, except for our sight. Awareness. Awareness. Awareness. Questions made the way back easier. Was the smell of Lake Michigan to the left or the right of us? Did we turn onto a paved smooth road? Working with another person could be a strength or not. It all depended on whether our emotions hindered our thinking process. Could we stay focused, each person's awareness helping the other. Half the night we wandered as scared bunnies with warm feet heated by the dunes' thermal sand. We made it back to camp, feeling a deep sense of power, even though we were terrified, frightened white rabbits.

Now it was my turn to use these scouting skills to make a path to my tent. I smiled to myself. This was going to be fun. All around were deer and cattle bones. They would be my guide. Ribs, femurs and jaw bones would point the way and I laid the trail in the afternoon sun.

Soon, Sunset Magazine colors filled the southwest sky. The colors were shattered by the sound of the Buffalo drum. There was a stampede toward the dance site. Full of hope, I started dancing on my right foot as evening stars began to appear in the azurite sky.

When Joseph decided to end the dance that night, the stars had turned into blue prisms of crystals reflecting white light from a thousand years ahead of our time. Heading to the tent, I stopped at the bonfire.

Relaxed and tired, my vision focused on nothing. For a moment, the flames became dancers. I called them Koo Wa Chee deer dancers. They wore masks of deer skulls and painted their bodies with earthly blood. These dancers were sacrificing part of themselves in another dimension, so we might witness them now. To see a world walker, demands the body and senses be elastic. The space between the cells is so vast, bigger than the Indian Ocean. You can sail in between the ocean of consciousness when the winds were right. "Some might say it's all in your mind, Druskis." And in some way, they were right. A rueful smile crossed my face. Out here on this land, events were happening never seen by the normal eye; only felt and experienced in collective recollection at a later date. Who is witnessing this wonderment? I shuddered with confused disbelief, as my body turned and walked towards the green tent. Following my bone trail was easy and falling into the unconscious abyss was a no brainer.

CHAPTER FIVE

"After One Comes Two"

After one comes two. The sun rose and it was the third day of the dance. I was finished, I wanted to go home. I was afraid of the throwing myself on the ground like a three-year-old and having a fit. A grand mal supermarket fit: step one, hold your breath until you turn blue; step two, fall onto the cold marble floor without hitting your head; step three, look into the eyes of your mother with pleading disbelief. Your mother will be too embarrassed not to comply with what you want. My mother would comply, with total frustration in her heart, she asked herself, "How could my immigrant child act this way? I've tried so hard."

How did the poem go, "Water, water everywhere, but not a drop to drink?" Drinking anything was not allowed. This process allowed the body to detox and the mind to clear. Drinking water would spiral the spirit back into the body and the focus would again be on the form.

"You're going to die this very minute. This really is bad for your kidneys," said my bitter tongue, as it shaped these condemning thoughts in my mouth, which all tasted salty with resentment. I had never gone this long without food or water. My ego was lecturing me on this very fact. "How are we to exist without form?"

When I finally succumbed, I held my breath, started to cry, and became lightheaded. This technique would not work here. Maybe in the supermarket with my mother as a child, but this was now. Concentrating on doing something in present time helped my mind stay out of trouble. Making the morning fire became the focus. My senses were engaged in this moment: smell of the fire, sound of the wood burning, feeling the coarseness of the splintery wood. Melting into the present, my awareness shifted and expanded.

While awareness amplified, my body was having trouble functioning. I didn't know if I could trust my body to make it through the day. I was not used to all this information my senses were bringing in. On reflection, I didn't trust my body. I was hitting another physical barrier, things inside were breaking down. It was time to throw myself on the ground give up and cry, I didn't care. All this little girl wanted was a teeny-weeny glass of water.

Then they appeared. The two most uninhibited creatures I had ever seen. Joyfully prancing, dancing, jumping over each other. Licking the air and kicking up their heels. They were darting left and right, oblivious to where they were going, I was caught in a time capsule. Frozen, watching the two young fawns nearly run me over. They stopped dead in their tracks when they saw me. This human. Was I to join them, came the question in their minds, as they tilted their heads with amazement. Cautiously, they moved toward me and sniffed. They seemed perplexed by my inability to move. Not waiting for my response, they leapt into the bushes in unison. A few seconds later, their proud mother crossed the river to join her children. Last was the father, with huge antlers. He was a majestic animal. With a slight turn of his imperial head, he surveyed his kingdom. All was right, there was no need to hurry on this sacred journey.

Wide-eyed, I drank the spectacle of life in front of me, feeling fed, knowing whatever happened this day, I would be taken care of. I wiped my eyes with my hands and then licked them. I wasn't going to waste any natural water at this point. I stared at my Reeboks for the longest while, and then muttered to myself, "They should be bronzed after this dance." They hold so much energy. A delirious smile crept across my face as I looked down at the clay earth. Around my shoes, yellow corn meal energy was emanating. I had felt this very energy in only one other place, at the upstate New York commune. Fairies were everywhere on that land. They wouldn't let a person be. They were great fun. My little girl came out to play with them as I started skipping on the path toward the dance arena. Where was my place, I wondered?

When I got to the dance floor, everything changed. Nearly everyone dancing was in a stupor. A collective screaming voice pierced my left ear from within, "How are you going to make it through the day, Fuck face?" it asked. A defiant teenage voice answered, "I don't care!" If I panicked and listened to my seemingly rational self, I knew I was going to die. I smiled at the group. It's simple. "The world around me is a mirror of my interior life. We are all one reflection."I whispered to my feet. "Courage," I said, as my right foot jumped into the circle of cedar branches. It was still the second day of dancing.

The end of that day left me feeling uneasy, on edge. I was not going to my dream state with any sense of adventure, only dread. Procrastination wrapped a blanket around the fearful little girl who had appeared. I stopped by my neighbor's twice to remind him to wake me if I overslept after a fitful night. As I zipped my sleeping bag, mother Owl started to hoot, and I thanked her.

Six a.m. marched around my eyelids and somewhere my psyche stood at attention while the rest of me slept. Finally, I jumped up with the strangest sense that my three-person tent would collapse and suffocate me. Gasping, I quickly unzipped the tent flap to crawl out. Thirst controlled my every thought. Yet something had changed.

Besides my normal emotional self, there seemed to be another being present as well. Some sort of witness. I could feel its formlessness and ability to quietly observe. This was my reflective self. It allowed me to watch my actions – crawl from the tent, take off my pajama bottoms and begin the great hunt for the perfect place to urinate. It was intriguing to observe this stout 40-year-old woman gingerly walking barefoot in the tall grass, half-clad, searching for comfort. All at once, she would disappear into the greenery, her head bobbing up and down like a Connecticut gray crane. Swear words spilled out of her mouth and onto the shallow valley like water. Then, red-faced, she would complete her morning ritual by wiping her ass and the inside of her legs with soft Charmin tissue. At first, she did not seem to enjoy this task. She did not want to soil her sacred Reebok shoes. On this final morning, however, she decided to take no chances. She wore neither pants nor shoes during her morning ritual. Upon reflection, her actions indicated her growing adaptability toward her awkward body. The only thought that kept her going on this final morning was that somewhere in this state was a McDonald's.

Before hearing the call of the drum, my reflective self fled, and I walked alone to a small creek on the reservation. As I gazed at the water, a thought floated by: what if there weren't any civilization past what you could see? What if your past disappeared right in front of your eyes? Mother told me the story of how she left Estonia for a graduate internship in pharmacology. The train was leaving for Tubingen, Germany. My mother leaned out the window, waved to her proud parents and then watched her whole world die. Over the hills came the Russian tanks to capture, destroy and conquer. She made it out of the country, never to see her parents or homeland again. The train never stopped until it arrived in the Fatherland at the deportation camps. "All gone. All new. Carpe Diem. We had to seize the moment in order to survive." My mother would tell me, as she inhaled cigarette smoke to cover the screaming in her lungs.

What would it take to separate from the horrors of life and just be in the moment? I walked to the river and meditated. Then I started to listen to the river. My ears became my mouth as I drank in the water through sound. When I walked up to the dance site, my mind was very quiet. The analytical part of myself had finally broken down, the tapes had stopped running. At last, I could hear my breathing, my heartbeat and my walking. The most important activity was staying in the present moment. By mid-morning, we had worked up a sweat from dancing. Joseph raised his hand and the drums stopped. We were finished. It seemed anti-climactic, but I was glad. My body had started to shut down, becoming cold and clammy to the touch.

When the dance finally ended, Joseph performed the water ceremony.

It was our first drink of water in three days. We were instructed to take only a few sips of water or stomach cramps would take over. Joseph's brother, Benito, blessed me. I drank water from a glass canning jar. I'll never forget how the water sparkled through it. Rolling the water in my mouth for the longest time, I wanted to remember that sensation for a lifetime of gratitude. Under a tree, I laid my body down and yearned for deep sleep. The thought was very short-lived, when Peggy, one of Joseph's helpers, walked over. Looking very tall from where I was lying, Peggy crossed her arms and whispered, "Joseph wants you to help prep for the celebration. Cook, for God's sake."

I stared up at her in sheer disbelief and gasped, "I don't bake, cook or prep food!"

"You will now," she turned on her heels and left.

As I walked toward the kitchen, I had a feeling someone was calling me. "I'm coming!" I shouted out loud. I'm hearing voices and they aren't mine. Mental telepathy, how easy can it be. I might as well drop all the inhibitions and use this skill of mental telepathy. "I'm coming as fast as I can."

The path to the kitchen wound around the Kiva-like structure through a small patch of sage bushes and a meandering line of pine trees. Looking up the hill, the first thing visible was a huge plastic water tank which supplied the entire encampment. Next to it was Joseph's white trailer. I stopped at a water bucket next to the door of the trailer. Putting my hands into the cold water, I splashed water on my eyes and face. Making a toothbrush out of my left index finger, I rubbed the inside of my upper and lower left jaw. Now I was ready to work.

Opening the trailer door, a woman with salt and pepper hair smiled and said, "I'm glad you came so quickly, I was getting impatient." She gave me a Goldie Hawn smirk, "I was practicing my mental telepathy. Did you hear me?"

"I heard you."

It was delightful to be among people who accepted our extended senses as being normal. It seemed logical that a group of people would start to use more of their psychic skills as they stayed together in harmony and kept cleaning their bodies. But along with the good stuff comes the shit as well, until you learn psychic discernment.

"Why do we have to follow the directions of this kid And why is he telling us what to do ? I've cooked for 30 years. I've got two kids his age at home," wailed the salt-and-pepper-haired woman. Her eyes were beginning to bulge with resentment.

Before I could shrug my shoulders in reply, the screen door swung open and in marched the Master Chef looking like the Pillsbury Dough Boy, baked by the Colorado sun. "I heard that. I'm not deaf. I am telepathic." With his pudgy fingers, he punctuated the hostile air and designated where the vegetables should be cut, washed, and sautéed. "And the dishes are on the upper right-hand shelf."

"Spunky little kid!" I thought to myself.

"I hate it when grown-ups call me a kid!" He glared at us, while waving a carrot. Upon second thought, I always felt it would be delightful to be among people who have developed their telepathic skills, except when my thoughts were involved. When Joseph asked us to do something, there always was a purpose. Something to learn. Kitchen detail was no exception. There, in front of me, was the male child as leader. I learned how to follow without too much judgment.

The first order of business was to make a pepper and eggplant salad. I was one of three-Sous chefs. Our job was cutting up: eggplants, red onions, green bell peppers. Someone brought Swiss chard from their garden. It needed to be washed and the white stems removed. Chickens had been roasted the day before and someone said there would be sacred Buffalo

Stew. Within half an hour a sense of trust started to flow in my veins. What metaphor was this boy showing me about my male side? My body relaxed with this question inside me and I focused on cutting up vegetables. Quickly the kitchen was filled with the aroma of a five-star gourmet meal.

The ceremonial feast was a total success. When we started to cook, I had figured, no one was going to criticize our culinary skills. These people hadn't eaten in three days. It didn't matter what we cooked, they would love it.

And so it was.

We were scattered outside, eating under the fur trees, digesting in the shade while the dogs sniffed for leftovers. Water was being treated like Dom Perignon 48' to be sipped slowly while savoring every drop. Joseph raised his hand and asked for our attention.

"First, I want to introduce you to someone who wants to share a story. She comes all the way from Philadelphia."

A tall slender woman in a long brown skirt stood up and walked to the center of the human circle we had created. She seemed shy and yet eager to share. "I'd like to share this dream of mine with you. This is what happened: I went into a deep dream state, then I got up and wrote it down. Becoming tired again, I went back to sleep, went into a light dream state to finish what I was doing in that realm and woke up to write down the rest of the dream. This went on for three nights straight back home in Pottstown. The first time I woke to write part of the dream, it seemed like I was dreaming with a group of people."

Folding my hands behind my head, I listened intently. This is what I heard and the response of the dancers to her dream, it will always be embedded in my mind.

"My dream came in segments," said the woman from Pottstown, "as I explained. I call it a creation story, because that's what it was. You know; there was God and he was perfect, but he was lonely. So, he created Adam and Eve. In my dream they came out of a delicate, phosphorus mint green moss-covered box. They were very happy living in the Garden of Eden. To me it wasn't on earth, it was somewhere else, and everyone was in a state of Bliss. Until one day together they found an apple tree and ate from it. They started to change, and God recognized this. In fact, everything around them started to morph and change. Everything: the trees, animals, the clouds above. This saddened God and he called the wondrous children to Him. "My dear, precious Eve and Adam; by eating the fruit of this tree together, you have started an amazing, irreversible process. I tell you that nothing will ever be the same. Because of your actions, change will be your constant companion. Everything around you will have a season. You will grow, age and die." The dreamer took in a deep breath and let out her breath in groups of words, "The apple represents time, not sex. There was no judgment placed on their actions. The creation story wasn't laced with sin.

The next part of my dream began with Adam and Eve starting their own family on earth. They descended onto earth the same way Dorothy did. Dorothy of the Wizard of Oz, you might have remembered her? Except in the whirlwind activity, they passed Kansas and landed in Idaho. I have a very vivid picture of their farm in Idaho. There was this two-story house painted eggshell white, with a porch that curled around the front and two sides. It sat on six acres of neatly clipped grass. A wooden fence, about knee high, separated the property from a deep emerald green forest. There were three bedrooms upstairs filled with children and I had the feeling the whole house was wallpapered in rose colored contentment, except for this one little, itty, bitty, question that kept niggling into Adam and Eve like a worm in their apple. Almost every evening they would come out on to the porch and sit on the swing. Eve would hold Adam's hand in hers, and once in a while, she'd trace the lines on his palm, as if to discover a pathway to their beginning. 'Where do you think we came from?' They would simultaneously look up into the starry sky, with heart-felt longing.

It was one of those evenings. While the sun was setting, a reflective white mist began to rise up from the forest. It was rolling like a bowling ball toward their picket fence. The couple were mesmerized watching the mist whirl toward them. Through the thick fir trees, over the picket fence and onto their neatly mowed lawn. What they couldn't see was a force riding on top of the milky mist. It hit them straight on. Faster than light could travel, the sound shattered all images in Adam and Eve's heads. The vibrations felt like someone was beating a hollow sequoia trunk with a huge stick. The tremor went through the interior of their heads. All DNA pictures of human history were destroyed in one spine-splitting THUD. Their minds were cleared of everything, and yet they moved forward looking west then east. For one irresistible instant, time stood still, so that perception could be surrendered. Nothing came or went in that moment. With the upward spiral of wind in the north shot another vibrating THUD and again emptiness. An eternity passed, then a majestic buck jumped onto the lawn. He was wearing a jacket of moss. He had cleaned off his antlers, by hitting them on the fir trees, and velveteen green moss fell onto his back. He pranced over the lawn, north-by-northeast and vanished. Shaking their heads in disbelief, Adam and Eve gazed upward for clarity, and suddenly, they got it, the whole meaning of their life. The why. The where. The lady from Philadelphia sat down into a heap made of her skirt. Quietly she folded her hands in prayer. "They realized that their longing was to know God again, which was right there inside them. Somehow the sound represented The Word. God."

As she sat down, a couple from the northeast is of the circle got up. They were holding hands. The man was stout and wore a beard. His wife seemed shy and retiring, yet there was an elegance about her. "We'd like to respond to your dream, if everyone doesn't mind?" For a big burly man, his voice sounded like a pleading little boy who needed his father to hear him. "You see," he stammered, "That woman has been describing our life in Idaho. I mean, we lived that dream. Or she dreamt us somehow." He stopped and then stuttered, "That was our house. The way we used to swing on the porch. Marilyn would hold my hand and ask me where we really came from. She saw right about Judith's bedroom. Judith's our oldest of five. The rose-colored room was hers. That buck. That was all true. The whole thing happened." They both sat down again in unison. Everyone was stunned. Little did we realize that an energetic web of creative consciousness was being revealed.

I unfolded my hands from behind my head and let my head rest on the earth. Remembering my dance, I uttered the words again, "Who is watching? Who is doing?" The questions were simple, my mind was complicated. The smell of sage blew up and around the hill. Its aroma filled the quiet crowd with wonderment, while Joseph smiled his coyote smile and flies stood perfectly still.

"He's done it again." I said to myself. Joseph is one of those teachers who shows us spiritual laws by direct experience. "Yeeees, sir reee, Bob! We were the mystery." I chuckled to myself. Several times before when Joseph would give a talk about the dream realm; someone's dream was another person's reality. The first time this happened, I was skeptical. Now it was a reminder that we are all connected somehow. I looked down at my hands and thought of John Daido Loori at the upstate New York Zendo, "Is not the left hand connected to the right."

My mind started to wander because of the heat. Thoughts and people began to trample in and out of my mind, as I lay on the ground. The Sioux Elder, White Deer, came into my vision and whispered, "On a day like this," with a crackly, dry desert smile, "The sun gonna burn a scorpion tail to black. Them lizards coming out on the rocks are baked. Now, you could eat those lizards and put the scorpion in tequila. But they don't go together." Then he would laugh.

Too much information, I thought. I was beginning to lose my sense of reality. For the first time today, I couldn't catch my breath. Trying to stand, my body doubled over with my left hand around my stomach. Needing help, my body headed toward Joseph's trailer; as my mind followed cautiously.

The trailer was full of people talking, eating, singing. In my mind, it was a flashback to the 60s, stepping over bodies at a rock concert. "Happy, Happy, Happy, but I didn't smoke pot." My gall bladder was dripping with unknown bitterness. I had to find a place to sit or to fall down. I yearned to be part of the crowd. Sally Perry caught my eye. She was sitting in the corner, savoring a piece of Indian fry bread smothered in butter and hummus. "Sally, move over. I'm starting to hyperventilate. It's all so unreal."

"Here, sweetheart, lie down on Joseph's sun dance blanket," she said, and unfolded it and patted it with the palm of her hand. She looked at me as if I was a golden retriever that needed to follow directions. "That will get you started," she chuckled. "Enough light in that to cut through twenty lifetimes. Miguel, come over here and help grab her feet. She's gonna start processing any minute now. Try and ground her the best you can."

There I was in a sea of people, flat on my back, flopping around like a beached whale. I was too exhausted to feel humiliated.

Sally put her long slender right hand on my forehead and a cooling sensation trickled downward from head, to neck, stomach to toes. "Your third eye is wide open, dear. Come on, can you hear me?" I shook my head as I listen to her talk like the Southern Belle telephone operator she was 29 years ago, "Close that third eye if you can."

I could hardly hear her. Gasping for air, my heart was pounding in my ears and waves of energy passed through me. My eyelids flashing Morse code pictures of some past life. If I could only focus on them. Sally put her dance blanket on top of me, tucking the edges under my chin. I resisted her caring efforts by trying to move my legs, so I could get up. Nothing worked. I laughed in disbelief, "I can't move!"

Sally's right eyebrow shot up and she barked, "You're not supposed to. Lay still."

Time flew, the flailing and discharging of energy seemed to go on forever. Finally, I finished with an extended gasp and elbowed myself into a sitting position. Sally cupped her hand on my back and lifted a moth for me to see. "This little fellow is going to be important for you. He is your guide for now. My guides are telling me that an issue that has been bothering you is being healed behind the scenes. The solution is ingenious, creative and will be a happy surprise for you in three weeks. The moth has come to tell you this."

The dusty brown moth sat comfortably in her palm. I laid him down on the Sun Dance blanket and received the moth from Sally. The moth stretched his wings while his eyes darted from left to right. My pleasure with him dissolved as pictures of an Egyptian temple crossed my mind and sank into my lungs, creating chest pains from suffocating. "I'm suffocating."

"You're right here." Miguel tightened his grip on my legs and my head fell back onto Joseph's blanket. "It's only a past life experience, girl. Let the pictures come. It's out of the past. You're not suffocating. Breathe deep."

Behind my eyes, pictures of a crypt flickered on a memory screen. The sketches pulsated to the rhythm of my shallow breathing. Hyperventilating again, I saw myself being buried as a craftsman, who had worked on the finishing touches of a religious text on my Master's coffin. Symbols were being placed on top of my mummified body for healing in the afterlife. A voice spoke softly, "You will meet him, Ibrahim. The Egyptian from Alexander. You will meet him in a future life. Ibrahim Karim. Remember his words well. He will come to you in California. The earth will move, and you need his knowledge."

Then another set of pictures passed across my mind: a ring was being placed in my hand by a fuzzy brown-haired saint by the name of Satya Sai Baba. His fashionable orange robe created an aura of glamour around him. I opened the palm of my hand and gazed at the simple 18 karat gold ring. It was old European gold, reflecting a tinge of pink as I turned it over and over with my fingers. "There will be many. They are to be found and given away, making the circle complete. None are for you in this lifetime." At that moment, I felt a huge pressure on my chest. Gasping for air, sweat dripping from my forehead, my spirit jumped back into my body and out of the vision. I sat up exhausted.

Sally looked deeply into my beady red eyes, which had lost any blue coloring. "Welcome back!" she said. She often spoke in an ordinary, lilting Southern voice, even when extraordinary events had happened. I found her southern drawl irritating as hell.

That sandpaper feeling found its way back into my dry mouth. My awareness crept swimming into different parts of my body. I heard my tongue rubbing up against my pallet. Then I bit my tongue and the taste of blood brought me further back into my body in present time. Joseph was walking around the group, listening and smiling. Then he came over to where I was lying on his Sun Dance blanket. I blinked, and he was in two places at once; here at the dance and in the Manhattan apartment.

I rubbed my eyes and squinted to see Joseph standing next to me in the Manhattan apartment. "Are you back from the future." He winked and smiled, "Already finished the dance and it hasn't even happened. That was my blanket." He whispered in my ear.

I turned in my chair to see the other members of the group staring at me. Sheepishly, my crimson face revealed my embarrassment. I had not mastered being in two places at once. That would take being totally in the moment and I wasn't there or here. I had fallen asleep listening to him and was dreaming the future.

Joseph turned away, finishing his talk on ceremony. Then, with raised hands, he invited us all to a dance at his place on the Ute reservation in

Durango, Colorado. "It's called a Drum Dance. And remember. If you sincerely make the commitment. Well, the dance starts the moment you do." Joseph's twinkly eyes took in everyone. He drew our minds back into this reality in a single breath.

A shriek came from the bathroom and Shrodinger the cat, ran out of the bathroom as if he, too, was returning from some unified field that had united gravity, electromagnetism and nuclear forces. How undignified!

It was almost midnight in Manhattan when we shuffled out of the small apartment, going our different ways. The quickest, shortest and economical route was the subway. The D train went to Park Slope, Brooklyn. Home. It never bothered me to travel so late after his talks. People were always on the train. This was shift change for the cleaning ladies. Half of the Russian countryside was crammed into the D train tonight. Short, fat women, wearing faded red checkered babushkas. They were squeezed three in a seat, it gave them a sense of security. We were riding in the belly of hell toward our forgotten homes. The older ones tried to speak softly, but their past never allowed it; "Prashna nuchka, mathca fuck him!

I grew up with the sound of different languages in my ear; intention being understood more than the words. "Prashna nuchka, mathca... translation: he was drunk last night, fuck him!" It was all music to my ears.

CHAPTER SIX

"Opening the Western Gate"

In some traditions, the direction of the East stands for the dawn, new beginnings, the mind. The West represents the physical, symbolized by the bear. It is the direction of the setting sun and the unconscious. Joseph had imparted a great deal of knowledge to us in Manhattan. Now it was time to actualize and integrate it into our lives the best we could.

I had decided to move to the west coast. When I told this to Joseph, a big smile crossed his face. "You may consider building a sweat lodge when you get out there." He never looked me straight in the eye, that was to intimate.

Say the vowel O and add hi. Long O and short i. As if you were just passing by and saying a friendly, "Oh, Hi!" That is how my mother pronounced it. It was a greeting: a light-hearted wave of the hand, the cupping of her hand and a joyous outburst of "Oh-hi" in her Estonian accent. She loved saying "Oh-hi".

That is where I moved to: Ojai, California.

Ojai, California is to spirituality what Silicon Valley is to present day technology. The town was a hot bed of spirituality since the twenties. Starting out with the Krotona Library built by the Theosophy Society. The Theosophy Society came out of Hollywood and landed in this East West valley. Even Krishnamurti built his famous library on the north end of Ojai. There were as many yoga centers, as there were bars, everything seemed sacred in Ojai.

This eponymous valley is nestled up against the Topatopa Mountains. Looking at the ridge of these Mountains, the view of an Indian Chief 's head appears. He has watched the development of this small valley for the past thousand years. Twentieth Century Fox found the mountains so enchanting, it became the backdrop for the movie "Shangri-La."

The energy in this valley runs East to West. There are three other valleys like this in the world and this East West energy flow allows for a certain consciousness to rise up. This refined energy slows the human system down, making it a perfect setting for spiritual communities to flourish.

For me, time began to flip like a nickel. On one side the spiritual buffalo picture: time began to accelerate; on the Jeffersonian side, time was uncomfortably slow. No one had heard of the "New York minute" in Ojai. I had to learn: the slower you became, the faster your awareness would accelerate, allowing for more conscious activity.

The week before moving to Ojai, I attended a sweat lodge in Los Angeles, praying for guidance concerning Joseph's suggestion to build a sweat lodge on the land in Ojai. He never demanded, just suggested. "It might be a good idea if you wanted," then he would hold his breath for a second, "to build a lodge when you move in the direction of the West." They were words said in passing, directly aimed at my heart. So of course, I would build a sweat lodge.

When praying in a sweat lodge, it is important to be very careful with your choice of words. Be decisive, clear in your intention and honest in your heart. Time has no bounds in any direction while sitting in the womb of the Lodge. The Great Spirit answers each prayer instantaneously. It is us, poor mortals that deal with timing and the awareness of our answered prayers.

It happened that way. Before boxes could be sorted out, unpacked and neighbors met, he appeared. Fred Wahpepah was a Kickapoo-Sac and Fox Elder and he answered my prayers. I will never forget his arrival. Fred Wahpepah was an Air Force man. "We do the impossible everyday" was the Air Force recruiting slogan. His men and women didn't mess around. He trained them hard and long. Nothing got past him, and he had eyes in the back of his head, like any good teacher. While the willows were being cut, fire pit dug, blankets smudged, stone people unloaded, Fred sat talking to the people, smiling and joking. But nothing got past him. "Wolf," that was Fred's adopted son, he had many sons, "Dig that pit deeper, because of the wind out here. Steven, are you starting the Fry Bread? And who is taking care of the prayer bundles? Can you show Ginger how to make them good and tight? Pipe carriers come over here."

The face of the Chief on the Topatopa mountains smiled down on us. For three years every lodge was a miracle. The word was out, and a multitude of nations came to do their ceremonies in this lodge. Each ceremony was different, but to Mother Earth, all was sacred. I watched as carefully as my heart could allow.

One afternoon, when the sun had kissed every orange in the south most orchard, in walked Marta. She was from the Tarahumara Tribe of Copper Canyon, Mexico. We were kindred spirits and didn't know it. But slowly, we supported each other in our spiritual efforts as teachers. We shared the knowledge and love of the sweat lodge as a "path" for spiritual growth.

In the spring, Marta was leading a workshop in Dream Journey. She was skilled at guiding people through their inner vision quest. She was a short, stocky figure that could move quickly when coerced into playfulness. The ancient wisdom of the Tarahumara was stored in Marta's olive eyes. She told me that her grandmother wore those eyes when she was alive and gave them to her upon her death. Marta was a very serious Shaman. Between us, trust ballooned into comfortable laughter as we grew to accept each other's dark olive side.

The workshop lasted for six weeks. Each week her students would lie on the floor of my living room, wrapped in comfortable blankets while she led us on an inner vision quest. I shouldn't say we. Her students were lead on an expedition of their psyche and I just slept. Understanding the deeper learning pattern was only reason she didn't kick me out of her class. To the other students, I was missing everything. To Marta, the only thing I was missing was some manners. She was polite enough not to wake me while snoring, which I did every week. Always upon wakening, there was such disorientation and disappointment of not remembering a thing.

"Listen Marta!" I puffed up my body, taking my thirteen-year-old tom girl stance, trying to explain my way out of the childhood embarrassment of snoring. "Some great people used the 'sleeping' technique to channel insightful information. Benjamin Franklin, was always falling asleep in the Continental Congress. The story goes he would wake up with a snort and say profound, relevant statements, that would surprise everyone; even Thomas Jefferson. Edgar Casey would lie down, fall asleep and begin to channel information for his clients. It never bothered him that he couldn't remember what he had said. His secretary recorded everything in shorthand. He was the 'Sleeping Prophet'. What about Thomas Edison? He would go to his favorite rocking chair, put a stone in his right hand and go into a trance. When this happened, the rock fell out of his hand and would wake him. This was his signal to start writing down the first thoughts that came into his head. Look at what he discovered! Bada bing. Bada bang!" I clapped my hands for a little drama.

"I can't remember a thing." I said softly, bowing my head in shame.

"You! What do you remember, after all the snoring? Where did you go?" Marta and I were about to have a Mexican standoff.

But then, during the very last class it all changed. Marta led the guided meditation, I fell into my usual deep sleep; except something happened when I awoke.

"Where in the hell are the Santa Cruz islands? How in the hell am I going to build a sweat lodge on an island? What is a Western Gate?" Obviously, hell was a familiar place for me and the questions came out in one full-throated snort.

The picture in my head was too large for me to comprehend in that moment. It took ten years to realize the ramifications of this vision. The event itself took only months to actualize in physical form. The steps seemed logical: get the people, go to the Santa Cruz Islands, build a sweat lodge, play the crystal bowls to open the Western Gate and go home.

It is always an auspicious beginning, when an abundance of money flows into the project. That abundance came in the shape of a man who wanted to join the expedition. This key player arrived from the back door. The door was facing west. But first, came the gifting from the sweat lodge with the door facing East.

Fred Wahpepah was holding a sweat lodge on the coast. Inside his lodge, I wailed, whined, and prayed for help on this project of building a lodge on the Santa Cruz Islands. After the lodge, I was approached by one of the other sweat lodge participants. Usually no one looks handsome after coming out of a lodge, but somehow, he did. I was impressed.

"Excuse me, are you the one who was praying about building a lodge on the Santa Cruz Islands?" He brushed his blond hair to the left side of his head and gave a grin that would have made Robert Redford take note for casting.

"Yes, that's me. God, what a project. I don't know where to begin." I was lost in Babylon and almost couldn't shut up long enough to listen.

"Maybe I can help. My family owns a rustic resort on that island. People come by boat or fly in to do hiking, hunting, that sort of thing. Would you like to see the island? I'm flying out next Saturday. I'd love to show you the lay of the land."

God always answers your prayers in the lodge. I wasn't looking for handsome, I was looking for help. I got both in spades.

The Santa Cruz Island is twenty-five miles off the coast of southern California. It is the largest of the California's eight Channel Islands. Feral pigs and sheep, descendants of domestic livestock had overgrazed the island and severely altered the natural systems and landscape at that point. The Santa Cruz Island fox and native bald eagles were facing extinction if they did not get help. The island's high peaks, deep canyons, pastoral valleys and seventy-seven miles of dramatic coastline beckoned us, n to come and explore.

Flying in the Piper Cub, we were low enough to see the shapes of the bottlenose dolphins swimming toward the island. I was delighted- like a child, until my adult eyes surveyed the island, looking for the landing strip, as we made our first pass over it. The plane tilted, and my nose pressed hard against the plastic window. Below, tall yellow grass covered the hills, bunches of huge red lava boulders were sticking out of the ground and there wasn't an airstrip in sight.

"I'm gonna bank it and land right over there. That area's quite flat." The pilot gave me a cowboy smile.

Now the little girl in me and my adult were sharing the same peak emotion: fear. I grabbed my seat and smiled as broadly as I could. After all he was doing me a favor by bringing me here or was this God's trick to announce my death. A vision appeared of the plane skidding across the grass and falling over the cliff into the ocean, right in front of the bottle-nose dolphins.

The one thing I learned about events that are peak moments in your destiny, they have three qualities: first the event is effortless. There is no resistance within your body, mind and spirit as you move toward your intention. Therefore, the amount of energy that you need to put out for the project is boundless and the world reflects this phenomenon with the path of least resistance. There is complete synchronicity. Secondly, the intended outcome is never what it seems. In retrospect, it is always larger than what the ego can perceive. For example, my main focus was to build a sweat lodge on the Santa Cruz island, but the larger intention had to do with the effect of opening the energetic Gate of the West.

By helping to open the Western Gate, it accelerated the energetic exchange between the East and West. Soon would come the western economic opportunities to outsource jobs to the East. To the West, Eastern thoughts and beliefs would flood America. The Dali Lama would be a house hold name. Delhi, India, would experience its first Western sweat lodge and the United Nations in New York City would have the opportunity to listen to one of India's highest sages: Yug Purush MahaMandeleshwar Swami Parmanand Giri Ji Maharaj. For ten years, he would humbly come to America and teach meditation with its purpose of wakening the Higher Self to those Americans who would listen. He also came to nurture the many Hindi communities across this vast America. Soon there would be an explosion of communication through the internet, cell phones, human awareness.

If the body, mind, spirit is in complete synchronicity with a larger consciousness, most often the person is catapulted to the next level of their personal growth. Which brings me back to the cliff.

The landing was effortless. There was only a small squeak, as the wheels hit the yellow matted carpet Mother Earth put out for us. The Piper Cub taxied slowly and gently stopped in front of a see through tin Quonset hut. Leaning against it were three weathered wicker chairs. On the ground near the hut was a sign in faded pumpkin orange: "Santa Cruz welcome ou." The "y" had been chewed on by some large animal needing their teeth sharpened. No bathroom, no water, no electricity, but it reminded me enough of civilization that I sighed with appreciation.

All at once from over the hill came the drone of two twenty first century scouts on their Yamaha Raptors. These four-wheeler trail bikes were meant for people who felt no pain.

Sean stopped and took off his head gear, to reveal a hungry, mischievous smile. "Come on. Sit behind me. Hang on ma'am. It's gonna be a little bumpy. We have 'til four o'clock before the helicopter arrives to get ya'. And we don't wanna be late for that." Jose, his partner, winked at Sean and they nodded in unison knowing full well, they'd love to see how this white woman was going to experience an overnight on the island. Obviously, there was little entertainment provided for the workers.

"O.K. Sean. I'm heading back to the Santa Monica airport. Take good care of Ms. Laima." Michael brushed his blond hair back, waved and jumped into the cockpit of the plane. In a moment, he was a dot in the sky.

I firmly believed that I was going to have to sign up for a kidney transplant, the ride was so stressful. What helped with the pain was the majestic view of the island and the peaceful Cyprus trees.

"See those horses? An olive farmer brought them over and just left them when he couldn't make a go of it here. They've survived four generations. Wild ones. Just let them be. They own the whole island, besides those wild pigs. They're wild too. Fittin' isn't it. Wild things." Sean was yelling at the top of his lungs. "Wild thing, I think I love ya!"

Three hours later, just around a bend, we dipped into an inlet where the beach almost touched the front door of a bunk house. It was the perfect beach to land a boat. Everything was going to be provided for us. Perfect.

When the helicopter picked me up at four, I knew everything would fall into place; except for one minor, major glitch. For me the project had to be blessed by the Awaswas Elders. They were known as the Santa Cruz people, one of eight divisions of the Ohlone. It was their sacred island. My vision had me doing a ceremony and opening up the energetic gate in their backyard. It's not nice to go into someone's backyard without permission.

Another month went by and almost everything was in place: space obtained on a boat, willows cut for the lodge, small plane chartered to bring the crystal bowls on to the island, so they could be played. People signed on to help with the project. All was well except for the Awaswas Elders. We needed their blessing to go ahead and there was nothing but silence.

Then one morning, a young lady broke the silence with a turnaround opportunity. An event that looks like a stop sign but really is painted in green and means do not hesitate but move forward with haste.

"Laima, I can't go. I'd love to. But. My boyfriend is coming from Hawaii and he's really in a bad way. Depressed. He needs some of my lovin'. I just can't leave him like that."

"So, bring him along." The words matched my thoughts, as I remembered we had extra funding. In my mind's eye he was the give-away. "It will be good for him."

"Yes, you're right. It would be very healing. You know he's Native."

"How Native?" Now I was listening very intently.

"His uncle is an Awaswas Elder." Bada Bing. Bada Bang. We have lift-off, Houston. My smile could be felt all the way to the other end of the phone.

"You mean he's seeing his Uncle, who happens to be an Awaswas Elder. Who happens to be concerned about his well-being."
"That's right, Jeffery always checks in with him when he comes to the mainland."

"Do you think he could do us a favor?" I squinted my eyes, to protect myself from any rejection.

"What d'ya want him to do?"

"We need this project to be blessed by his Elders. We need their prayers that when the gate is open, it will support the Highest Good for all humans. God, could we use some help connecting with our highest good."

As I was talking, my mind's eye flashed on arriving in America as a baby going through Ellis Island. My parents were fortunate, they met the American migration quotas for the country they were born in; my father was born in China and my mother in Russia. My mind saw pictures of the Statue of Liberty, pier 47 in Manhattan, and my mother holding me tight, as they looked out onto this vast city, full of opportunities.

"What d'ya say?"

"Nothing." I sputtered into the phone. I always had trouble double tasking. My mind was trying to connect some dots and speak at the same time. So it was, Creator provided for us, now we needed to move forward. "Wa ma chi." Joseph would sometimes mutter under his breath as we walked, or started to work, "Wa ma chi. Wa ma chi."

That is how our give-away became our blessing-way. Jeffery went to his Uncle and asked for his blessing on our project. What happened was most startling. Like our life being the metaphor of our greater self, Jeffery's meeting with his uncle was no different.

It was their custom to smoke pipe together, when Jeffery went to his Uncle's house. The ocean and life had separated them too long. Jeffery was now a tall, tan, troubled half-breed, needing the council of an elder. But with all his personal baggage, he honored the opportunity to carry our request for a special blessing to his Uncle. This was the Way. His tradition.

His Uncle listened as Jeffery told him about our project. How was it that a native of another land should enter their dream time and be called to open their treasured gate? Why was it a woman, when only men had guarded the gate for so long? What great winds would travel through the gate and who would it bring? All of these questions crowded his Uncle's mind, making his body uncomfortable.

His Uncle lovingly looked into Jeffery's eyes and saw it all. He prepared the area for this ceremony, by singing songs and burning sage in a conch shell. They both watched the smoke rise as the Elder smudged his cherished son. It took Jeffery a long while to make his body comfortable in lotus position. Then he was ready to share again. His Uncle, sat as still as a southern alligator lizard basking in the sun of their island dreams. Eyes closed, skin of leather, only his breath moved his stomach up and down, while he listened to Jeffery tell the tale of the woman who wanted to build a lodge on their island and make sounds from crystal bowls that would harmonize some things and let go of others. It was all a mystery that seemed so right to Jeffery and he didn't understand the parts but felt the whole.

After speaking, Jeffery dug into his pipe bag, while whispering a prayer to Great Spirit. The stem of the pipe was securely wrapped in red cotton cloth, for protection. The bowl was wrapped tightly in a crimson cotton cloth. Jeffery's mother had beaded his pipe bag with great love and symbols that would guide him and his pipe toward their Nation's highest good. Jeffery lifted the stem of the pipe, representing the male aspect of the pipe and said a prayer. The bowl, represented the womb; Jeffery closed his eyes in order to muster all the gratitude for his parents he could and then connected the stem into the bowl. At that very moment, his Uncle took the pipe and broke it in half. Both men gasped in pain with its implication.

"Here! It is broken. It is your duty to fix it. You must find a new way through your actions. The old ways will not work now. How are we to live together? Find a way or we will all die. Open the gate." That is all he said. There wasn't room for any more thoughts. Only songs for forgiveness could fill the air now.

Jeffery was dumbfounded. This was heresy. Never had he heard of such an action by an Elder. Shrugging his shoulders, he reminded himself that the whole project was unorthodox and yet there was a ringing of truth.

Then he heard the words, "I talk of the search for the truth hidden behind the mind. Truth never requires a veil. It is naked. It is very simple. The truth is open to all and meant for all." As Jeffery penetrated his mind with awareness, a flash of orange passed through his eyes.

And then the day came, like the waves, never ending, one after another. It was time to move forward toward our destiny.

CHAPTER SEVEN

"Know the Wave, Be the Ocean"

Eight of us boarded the charted boat that went to the island twice a week. As my crew stepped on board, I marveled at the talents each brought to the project. We were blessed to have Jock, the Ojai baker bringing lots of French bread from his oven. All the willows to make the lodge were provided by the natives who knew where they were growing in the nearby forest. They knew the ceremony of permission, to cut the willows in a "good way" and songs that were to be sung. They brought the willows. Joseph's brother had taught me the song to sing while looking for the lava rocks we would use in our lodge. Two other members of the project were flying in to bring the crystal bowls. The crystal bowls would be used to "sing" the western gate open.

All was provided for.

Half way to the island, a pod of bottlenose dolphins joined our cause. These dolphins frequently ride on the stern wakes of boats. This activity is probably adapted from the natural behavior of riding ocean swells. Their afternoon playfulness was infectious. Jeffery gathered us around to hear a story his Uncle had told him when he wa s very small and lived here on the mainland.

"The God's had told his people to make a long journey from the Island to the mainland. They would go to this mainland and all would be plentiful. They would never have to worry about food in this new land, if only they would have faith and make the journey to the vast mainland that never ended. The entire community prayed for protection on this adventure to their new homeland. The boats were built and then the stars were consulted for the exact day for them to start their journey.

The day came filled with anticipation and questions: could the boats carry them all safely to the other side? The Gods laughed and showered them with tears. As they paddled toward the mainland, it started to rain, the waves rose up and began to fill the boats with water. The Gods kept laughing and watched as the people rowed in horror. The sky became black. The waves rose up like sea monsters, mouths open. Old women cried, children hid their faces in their mother's breasts and the men rowed. The Gods looked on and said, "Remember when you go to this new world, there will be people of all colors. Learn to work with them. Only then will you be saved." One giant God waved his hand and a rainbow appeared. He picked up as many boats as he could and placed them on the rainbow, so they might reach the other side safely. Still some of the people fell out of their boats. They became the bottlenose dolphins that now live in the bay. Look, they are swimming with us now." Jeffery pointed to the pod of 13 swimming alongside the boat. Two of the dolphins jumped higher than ten feet in the air and landed on their backs, making joyous clicking sounds.

We all listened to Jeffery like children, while the dolphins jumped playfully in the recognition of their past. His story had a mesmerizing quality. Turning my head sideways I looked at the dolphins, playing with the wake of the boat. Could they be as intelligent as us? They were swimming in rhythmic patterns, when I noticed a shadow of a helicopter pacing the dolphins. I frowned and remember the navy base not far away. I had a natural distaste for the Navy because of a past life. I couldn't shake it. Cupping my hand, I looked up to scowl at the chopper. Something was wrong. The side door of the helicopter was open. Inside were the frames of two women waving; frantically trying to get our attention. They were wearing civilian clothes. "Nah, not JJ and Lisa! They were bringing the crystal bowls by helicopter." My disbelief was washed away by the ocean spray that met my face. "The Navy. That is a Navy helicopter, Jock? Right?" I turned my head to the other side, parallel to the water, for a better view. My perplexed mind remembered that JJ had put on a red jump suit this morning and it was not Navy regulation. One of the persons in the helicopter was wearing something very red and was very happy.

Now everyone was focused on the Navy helicopter circling the boat and then heading for the beach, where we were to land. I am sure we would hear the whole story within the hour, as everyone breathlessly watched the helicopter land on the beach. Then two Navy seals gracefully carried the women ashore to the dock and unloaded three hug boxes, making sure they would not get wet. When the boxes and the women, were safely put on firm land, the two Navy seals stepped back; gave a crisp salute, made a hundred and eighty degrees turn and trotted in unison back to the helicopter. The chopper promptly lifted straight up and then turned due West toward the afternoon sun.

"Why is it that you two are always upstaging me?" My shoes were wet from unloading our supplies onto the beach and then carrying them to The Scorpion Ranch bunkhouse, where we would stay. I was wet and tired.

"Upstaging you! It was a miracle." Crooned the two of them like teenage girls who had managed to borrow their fathers' pink convertible, keys in hand, with the top still down. Totally delighted with what had happened.

I closed my eyes to listen. "Well, since you asked. This is how it happened. We went to the airport and when we checked in, can you believe it! They didn't have us scheduled. Na Da! No plane. No pilot. Nothing. And no one was available. Except. Standing to the side was this handsome Navy pilot dressed to go. I mean to go. All smiles. Checking us out. I batted my eyes and took one step forward. He took one step forward. So, why not tell him of our plight, I thought to myself. I said in my, "little girl, come here, I am lost" voice. "We need to get these two-crystal bowls to the Santa Cruz Island today. Could you give us a lift?"

By this time their breathing had synchronized, and they took on The Diane Ross stance, lifting their hands straight into the sky and crooned, "The Navy! The Navy! From sea to shining sea. Wasn't it nice they carried us to shore?" From that moment on I promised God, He could work it out anyway She wanted. Who was I to judge the carrier of such important cargo. As Joseph said, "I only work here."

The next day, the sweat lodge was built in a grove of eucalyptus trees. To the Native Americans, the sweat lodge is like a Church. Inside the lodge, the body is cleansed and the soul can be healed. In other parts of the world, such as the Baltics, the sauna was used for certain ceremonies of the same nature. Here on the Santa Cruz Island, we built the lodge according to the teachings of Fred Wahpepah and Joseph Rael. Our prayers were focused on healing the planet, opening the western gate and our personal relationships.

After the lodge, our next goal was to find the exact point where the crystal bowls should be placed and played. It was easy to see where the gate was, when viewing it from the mainland, looking west. It was like the dip in a camel's back, on the east side of the island. Our guides had pointed out a trail that lead to a buttress that looked at the mainland.

Jeffery, his girlfriend and Jock's family decided to hike to that point. The rest of us loaded up the dune buggies with the boxed crystal bowls, blankets, food and water. We dressed warmly, it was a windy location.

When I got to the location, I took out my pendulum and began to find the energy grids. My thoughts ran to Ibrahim Karim, the father of BioGeometry. I was fortunate enough to attend several of his lectures on ancient links between energy systems, integration of science and spirituality and creating harmony within our inner and outer environments. It was Dr. Karim who taught me to use the pendulum to find the ley lines. Ley lines are energy pathways that run in and around the earth. This system around the earth, is akin to the meridians on the human body, which were charted by ancient Chinese schools of medicine. By placing the bowls directly on certain ley lines, the vibration of the bowls could be carried around the world. Our intention of connecting with this sight was to activate a certain harmonic vibration, in which the outcome would be to jump start certain connections. Envision Nikola Tesla's alternating currents, electromagnetic fields, the energizer bunny going on and on, and there I was. Quieting my mind and using the pendulum to draw a line in the sand. "Here, I said to myself, "Place the bowls here. No thinking. Just doing."

The crystal bowls were set a foot apart, my foam cushion gave my hips comfort as I sat in lotus position. I leaned forward and stroked the rim of the bowls with the leather covered rods. The friction between the leather and the edge of the crystal bowl produced a beautiful tone. One crystal bowl was larger than the other; each had its own vibration. When the vibration from one bowl met the vibration of the other, they created a harmonic sound.

The winds took the harmonic sound and gently pushed them on their way along the casual body of Mother Earth. I imagined a crystal shawl of alternating harmonic current being wrapped around Mother Earth's shoulders running East and West. The current would alternate like Tesla's coils, except these were made from crystalline sound.

That evening we took the sweat lodge down, leaving the land just as we found it. We packed in silence, allowing the pictures of this event to crystallize inside us as we went to bed. Now we were the bowls, shifting up to a higher vibrational rate of our personal karma.

Sunrise came and so did the boat from the mainland. The hard work of carrying: forty gallons of distilled water, four boxes of uneaten food, thirty-five blankets that covered the lodge, sixteen willow poles, twelve sleeping bags, ten suitcases, two crystal bowls, cameras, shovels, axes and one set of men's size eleven never-used scuba gear; gave each of us something to carry. We needed this task of "carrying" in order to ground us as we started to enter the journey of our seemingly ordinary lives.

CHAPTER EIGHT

"The Kiva Journal"

It was the summer of '94 and I was stuck in Hoboken, Frank Sinatra's home town. Every good Italian restaurant blared out his albums: "Only the Lonely," "Nice 'n' Easy." I had just moved back to the East Coast from California. I didn't have a clue concerning job prospects. Nothing was nice and easy. The word photography was stale in my mouth and I wanted to discover something new within me. What could be done with all this spiritual work? I could teach meditation, but make a living from it? No. Boredom was eating my psyche, it was showing itself in every pound I gained.

Self-pity wasn't working either. I needed help. It was time to call Sally Perry. Eight years had passed since the first Drum Dance on Joseph's land. Sally had traded in her million-dollar hair salon to become an internationally recognized healer. Joseph, was fulfilling his vision of leading dances and creating sound chambers around the world. They both were my teachers; their personalities balanced different parts of mine.

There was a strong teacher-student bond between Sally and me. With Sally around, I knew that my life was safe. More than once she had brought me back from the edge of other negative realities I had created for myself. Her gift to me was a shimmering net of White Light. My gift to her was the testing of her patience.

Whenever I telephone Sally, she is home. That is amazing, considering her travel schedule made any top CEO's itinerary seem sedentary. My trick for success, getting her every time I called, was to dial her telephone number internally. I put her name in my mind and if her name kept coming up more than three times within the afternoon, by five p.m., I knew she would be in.

I had started exploring my telepathic abilities several years ago when looking for photographic work. I chuckled, when a photographic client said, "We were just talking about you today. Funny that you should call." It was a nice introduction to asking for work.

Sally was home and we started discussing computers, writing, and after a few minutes, I felt comfortable enough to mention the stuck factor. She went directly into psychic reading mode. She took several deep breaths and said very softly, "I see a foot in your heart."

That was just what I needed to hear I had a shut-down heart. My heart was still in Ojai and I was in Hoboken. Sally's words seemed to put me in a trance. My mind kept drifting to the edge of the Topatopa Mountains, that lie in an east west direction of the Sierra Madre Mountains. The smell of chaparral filled my nostrils. Both hands twitched, as I rolled an imaginary sage bundle. "Are you listening to me?" She barked. "It has to do with your mother's side of the family. It's interesting that none of you girls had children. I see slavery and war."

It sounded about right for ninety percent of the Baltic history. My grandfather was an amazing businessman. He started several businesses in Estonia and each time a war came, the war destroyed everything and he would start again. I told Sally the story of my mother leaving Estonia and going to Germany to study pharmacology.

Mother kept repeating the story of when she boarded the train in Tallin. She had won a scholarship. Her parents were so proud. "Elena will intern at the best pharmacy in Tübingen." her mother would tell the neighbors over and over again. Her daughter got on the train, waved goodbye, with thoughts of coming home in the fall. Elena sat down in the comfortable first-class compartment. Her father had saved enough money, so the ride would stay in her heart forever. Elena looked out the window and, in an instant, watched her life change forever as Russian tanks entered the station and the train never stopped. It went to Germany. She never saw her parents or her country. Her beloved Estonia was gone for ever.

"What you need to do is sit in a Medicine Wheel. I see four days. One day for each direction. The traditional no food, water. You will have to make 405 prayer bundles for your family. Ask for forgiveness. Pray for abundance for your family. At the end, have something from your family for a giveaway and you may want to talk to Joseph before you do it."

That was very straight forward. Why not call Joseph. What was he going to say, "Good luck!" Of course, he would concur with Sally.

My first thought was to set up a medicine wheel in the apartment in Hoboken. "What do you mean, the meditation room in the apartment?" said my best friend and confidant, Barbara. "The dogs running around, the street noise from Ho...Hoboken. What happened to Nature?"

Advise taken, I called Betsy Stang, the director of the Wittenberg Center in Woodstock, N.Y. The Wittenberg Center is located in Bearville, New York, which is just around the bend from Woodstock. At the center, people could participate in sweat lodge ceremonies; explore ancient shaman techniques of travel using the drum; listen to lectures given by tribal elders; or quietly travel inward by spending time in the Peace Chamber, which was on the land. I negotiated the fee to rent the chamber for three nights and four days. Timing was critical.

Usually when I do spiritual work, the timing dovetails with other major events that I am not aware of until after the fact. But now I had a glimmer, it was going to be important for me to be in the Chamber when the comets hit Jupiter. This event would have a certain impact on the earth several years from now. Being in the Chamber while this happened, was going to have an effect on my work. July the 18th through the 21st was the target date. That weekend comets were starting to descend and Native America Elder, Running Horse was giving a workshop in the Chamber. I had a feeling the energy in the chamber would be electrifying and I might even get to meet Running Horse.

Before starting the Medicine Wheel, I decided to visit old friends in upstate New York. Virginia Cantarella was my landlady for eight years while I lived in Brooklyn. I am sure her husband, Herman Shonburns, was a lover, husband, or wife of mine in some other life time. Who knows? But it was love at first sight in this lifetime. When I saw Herman, I beamed. It was very rejuvenating to have people in your life that you loved unconditionally.

Herman was round, with sly, twinkly sky eyes that darted lightning fast to let you know his razor-sharp mind was about to strike. He was a man who had problems in life and worked on them diligently; making him a national treasure of resourcefulness and wisdom. He enjoyed the presence of good looking women and we delighted in playful conversation about the female species; which always lead us to commenting on his wife Virginia Cantarella. She was a strawberry blond, with a body that walked right out of VOGUE magazine. She is an artist, mother and most importantly to me, a family Elder. If eldership encompasses life experience, compassion, humor and the courage to listen without judgment; she could do it in spades with such finesse. Her Italian is impeccable, and her spaghetti is always served al dente.

Virginia had marinated a quart of artichoke hearts, drained the mozzarella, cubed the spicy pepperoni and halved the cherry tomatoes. She had started her magic. Herman and I would inevitably start a rabbinical discussion for the millionth time; what does "it" mean, as we set the table. Today, the "it" was realizing what a wonderful extended family I had. The body and mind were fed and so was the soul, al dente.

I didn't want it to end. But all things do. So, we made happy faces, while hiding the distance we were about to put between us. I got in my rental car and waved goodbye. Next stop, Woodstock. Traffic was going smoothly until the entrance to highway 85 and 90. For a moment, I became mesmerized and was pulled toward Massachusetts. The magnetic past was tugging me, but I resisted. I was trying to cover an hour and half of driving in 45 minutes. On the outskirts of Woodstock, traffic filed into one lane each way, as road repairs were being made. I tried to make my mind one lane and concentrate on the driving. In slow motion, I watched fences being erected in pastures, to create the American landscape called the parking lot, which was being dotted with portable potties. The town of Woodstock was being transformed to celebrate the 25th reunion of The Woodstock. Every shop window displayed fifty different t-shirts commemorating it. Did we really wear those tie-dye pants? I imagined herds of people moving toward some Nirvana, ready to sway in unison.

Before arriving, I had called the center making an appointment with Running Horse. We would meet after his seminar was finished in the chamber. The Wittenberg Sound Chamber is built part way into the earth. Its wooden roof is circular. At the center point of the roof is a plastic dome. The floor of the chamber is dirt, covered with pea gravel. A fireplace is recessed into the west wall. All around the circular chamber wall are crevices with room to place candles and crystals. Outside the chamber, the fullness of summer was everywhere. Tall, majestic fir trees surrounded the chamber. Not more than fifty feet from the entrance, a deer appeared. The deer stopped and decided to graze on the tall grass. She was undisturbed by our presence and movement.

Running Horse wore a forest green shirt that was buttoned to the top. It gave him an official air. His brown fedora felt hat was a Stetson. In his left hand, he twirled an eagle feather; the right hand held a wooden cane.

We walked silently to the Chamber. When we entered, a medicine wheel had already been created. Four huge white candles marked the four directions and a chair was positioned behind each candle. I pointed to the direction of the North and gestured that he might sit there. Running Horse entered the Medicine Wheel from the East. He then walked directly West in a straight line, as if to cut the medicine wheel in half. At the center of the wheel, he stopped, turned his body 360 degrees, and continued walking to the western edge of the circle, where he turned with a smile. He sat down on the wooden chair facing North. The chair was covered with a protective red colored Hudson Bay blanket. The blanket had two bold black strips at each end of it, which gave the blanket a sense of authority.

In my mind, I took note of his energy field. His male and female energy seemed to be balanced when using his cane. Sensing his openness, I was relieved.

I decided to be as candid as my heart and ego would allow. Tears welled up and I started to cry. "You know, Running Horse, it's really hard to see someone you have known for many lifetimes and not acknowledge that fact. It's good to see you again. A thousand lives are swirling around us. So paper thin are the entry ways. Most of us are sleepwalking, never seeing our ancestors, who speak without being heard."

Running Horse gave me a sideways glance, holding his breath for a moment, and then smiling compassionately as he exhaled.

"Sit, Running Horse. Isn't it enough in one lifetime, to have the presence of someone you love, shared in this way? Let us just sit and talk."

The air grew thick with our presence. Slowly, he began to tell me about his work, grandchildren, his coming death and friends he wanted to see before he passed over. We shared the fact that each of us had been working on different vortexes, the loneliness of our work and the great Mystery that follows us with Light.

The topic of healing the earth came up and I blurted out that there were many more Earth upheavals to come. I bent over and vomited the words, "In a twinkle of an eye, the Earth could be transformed. You and I have seen it: communities gone, fields instantly becoming the bottom of the ocean." I began to sweat in a sea of panic, as if it might happen any second.

Running Horse raised his left hand and twirled the eagle feather in the space between us, as if to zip up the entrance into the multi-dimensional world we had just witnessed. Leaning back into the chair, he closed his eyes and whispered, "What will you do here?" Sweat began to pour down his forehead. He wiped it away with his right hand. The chamber had become very humid and hot.

"A Medicine Wheel. Four days and three nights. I've never done one for that long," I said, trying not to show my anxiety.

"There is still much to be revealed about the Medicine Wheel," said Running Horse, speaking softly, while circumnavigating the Medicine Wheel with his eyes. He seemed cautious; after all, we had not met before in this lifetime. He was soft and wise, I was blunt and bewildered.

I cleared my throat and closed my eyes to see the mental list that Sally had given me. "The first day will be making prayer bundles for my ancestors and expanding it outward to others. I want to remember people from my family's past and make amends, so I can release them. I want to become lighter. Not carry around so much weight. The second day, I'll sit in the different directions, learning what I can about the Medicine Wheel and how it spirals into time and then...." I hesitated, as if everything should be known, but I didn't know and was ashamed, "I don't know."

"That's alright. Spirit will come," said Running Horse, as he smiled a vote of confidence, "You may be one of the few that will do some of the work that is needed. I will pray for you and bless the chamber. Do you have guides?"

"I am sure I do, but I haven't made a conscious...." My voice trailed off. "I haven't met them consciously yet." I knew it was not the right statement to be making. This acknowledgment was akin to my family doctor confessing that she failed in her anatomy course while in medical school, but was doing fine diagnosing only with her intuition.

"Hmmmmmm. You will need help." Running Horse said with a twinkle in his eye.

"Yes, I could use some." I shuffled my feet and began to smile. The next moment we looked at each other and roared with laughter.

Standing, he held the Eagle feather over my head and prayed in his native tongue. His words were sincere, they were filled with the roundness of vowels. When he finished, I slumped back into my chair; he did the same. My hands reached for my beloved ceramic Japanese bowl, given as a present while I was attending the inauguration of John Daido Loori as Abbott of the Zen Mountain Monastery. I cherished that bowl. Every time I picked it up, the feeling of the glazed sides ignited memories of him walking to each station outside the monastery during the ceremony. In my ears, the words of his haiku rained on a past pleasure field of time within. Cupping the bowl in my hands, I told its history to Running Horse. Then looking at my hands, I knew what else to give: my favorite rings. "I have a history of finding rings for people." Pulling them off, I placed them in the ceramic bowl that was filled with tobacco. "Here, Running Horse, these rings are a give-away. You will give them to those who are waiting."

Placing his feather in the bowl, he turned, "When should I give these rings away."

"When? Running Horse? You will know." I laughed again, letting tension release in the sound I made. Loved that man, don't know why, never met him before. My logical mind prattled on about synchronicity as he walked out of the chamber.

Suddenly, the image of Thackito Wahpepah and Joseph Rael came into my thoughts to comfort me during my preparation. They were my main teachers for the study of the directions, through the Sweat Lodge Ceremony. Joseph is a member of the Southern Ute Tribe of Ignacio, Colorado. His father was of the Picuris Pueblo Tribe. He was given his spiritual name, Beautiful Painted Arrow, by his grandfather. As a young boy, he was put in the Ceremonial Chamber to open up his vision; as a man, his vision on the Sun Dance floor became global.

Everyone knew Thackito Wahpepah, as Fred Wahpepah. He is an Elder from the Algonquin speaking nation. His mother was from the Kicka-poo-Sac Nation. His father was a Fox elder. Wahpepah means "Leader of Eagles." It's no wonder he joined the United States Air Forces. The man could give orders with lightning speed and he never missed anything while preparations were being made for a lodge. Fred has traveled all over the United States as a Sweat Lodge Elder. He was the architect of the sweat lodge we built in Ojai. I became the "keeper of the land." He has seen me through some fierce sweats and enjoys telling others about my low toler-ance for heat.

If Beautiful Painted Arrow was the elder who took me to other worlds, it was Fred Wahpepah who constantly reminded me to be conscious here and now. To me, Fred was the grounding rod into Mother Earth, and Joseph helped me to expand into other realms. The two of them made up the male side of my Council of Elders. Sally Perry and Virginia Cantarella represented the female part of my council.

Once at a sweat lodge mainly for Sun Dancers, the lodge was hot enough to burn your eyebrows. I kept hearing the phrase, "It's a good day to die," many times that day. It was a favorite comment often made by the men who were going to the Sun Dance this year.

Just before you leap into a ceremony, all your life force is summoned to perform the act of jumping into the present unknown, in order that some part of you can be released to death. This was one of those moments. It was time to jump into my ceremony and some part of me would die.

Trying to be grounded, I got the cornmeal that Marcie had given me for protection. I started in the East and moved clockwise around the inside Chamber wall. The walls were embedded with crystals. All around were sparrow nest ledges that could support candles. As I placed thirty thin, white candles around the chamber and lit them, the Chamber became a cathedral of fractured light.

The first preparatory step was to offer tobacco to each direction. As I picked up the tobacco out of my medicine pouch, I reflected on the fact that this was a substance that my family had abused and it ruled their lives until death. Now I was honoring the spirit of tobacco.

The first time I was offered tobacco to smoke in a "cha nup pa," during a ceremony, I exploded. One puff and every cell in my body seemed to expand ten-fold. The sensory upload was overwhelming. I had heard stories of people pulling themselves out of the grip of heroin but who were unable to stop smoking. I could feel a certain tug of addiction toward this sacred plant.

Then I continued the ceremony by standing in the direction of the East and began to pray:
"Father/Mother, help me to keep your light in my mind's eye. Bless this new dawning. Give me the courage to let go of the past to start anew. Great Eagle Spirit, carry the prayers you hear these four days to the Creator. Let me rise above my tangled habits of this lifetime and become the midwife to a new tomorrow." Then the tobacco was placed on the ground in the direction of the East. Turning to the South, I raised my arm up high to show all Beings this offering. "In the direction of the heart-felt emotions, let me plant the seeds of compassion and self-acceptance. Let us become lovers and develop the power to grow. It is during the night that You, Great Spirit, rise up to dissolve polarity while bathing in the moonlight of forgiveness. How many times during the waking hours the world was black and white, good or bad, my judgment separating any sense I might feel of connection. Oh, Great Spirit, let me put my head down and become one with you. And so, one became two."

The smell of tobacco filled the air as I threw it to the ground. "Spirit of the West, now I turn to you, Oh, Great Bear. One who knows the courage of introspection and reflection, during your hibernation. Only to be born again in Spring, come forth. Like the Bear with her large claws, let me dig for the roots of truth. With Her guidance, let the truth be known, more than just the reality of it. Develop my sense of awareness so that I may awaken to the consciousness that pervades everything." The tobacco seemed to be floating to the ground like new December snow. "Oh, Great Spirit, turn the wheel of Samsara to the direction of the North." This is where the Elders sat. Running Horse and Beautiful Painted Arrow were shining examples of courage and endurance. "Do not shelter me from the dangers of this world, Oh, Great Spirit, but give me the courage to face them. Let me have the heart to conquer my pain. Let me not always depend upon my allies in life's battlefield; but first, help me find the depth of my own strength. Let me not crave, like a spoiled child, to be saved from my fears. Give me Grace, oh, Great Spirit, with the patience to win my freedom from my illusions." Spreading my fingers, I watched the tobacco escape my grasp to land in the arms of The Mother. I turned and walked to the center of the wheel. "Mother Earth, Father Sky, let all my actions be directed through the heart and guided by the intellect." The last of the tobacco was placed at the center of the Wheel as I whispered, "One joins with two, two becomes three, three lies with fourth power, and then there were eighty-one."

I stepped out of the Wheel and looked at the two huge cardboard boxes I had carried into the Chamber when I first arrived. Inside were the family crystals. No goblets, just two crystal bowls. The largest being four feet high by three feet wide. I called them the family crystals, because I didn't have any family heirlooms. I came to America with two parents and one suitcase. Now I had a huge extended family and was given gifts to last several lifetimes.

These crystal bowls were made of ninety-nine percent crusted quartz that was heated to four thousand degrees in a centrifugal mold. Quartz crystals have many physical properties: amplify, transform, focus and transfer energy. They are used in radios, television equipment, and computers. Our bodies can be called "crystalline structures," because our bone marrow has silica in it. When playing the bowls, the sound made by the quartz crystals, resonates with the silica in our body. This affect relaxes and harmonize the physical form. The sound can have a positive effect on our cells to our large organs. I brought them to help me raise my vibration and transform the space. I placed one of them in the direction of the north and the other in the south, cutting the Medicine Wheel in half on energetic lines.

The third and final element was the unwrapping of the two owl wings that my sister Lee and I found from a road kill, on the sandy shores of Lake Michigan. She is my teacher in this lifetime, who prods me to take flight into the adventure of life. Lee loves to travel. In the Yucatan, Lee was my guide to Labna. There we would meditate about our future. I photographed the archaeological sites with my Widelux camera; she would climb every inch of rock to find me new glyphs to capture on film.

At Chichen Itza, I was fascinated by the Ball Court. The sport that was played on this field was simply called the "ball game," It was popular all across Mesoamerica. What interested us was the acoustics within the Ball Court; not the game itself. Joseph had peaked my interest in sound and vibration. We were in a perfect place to experience acoustics perfection. No one has cared to mention that this court has a perfect horizontal/ circular sound system. We played telephone. Standing on any corner of either wall; I would cup my hand and whisper into my palm, "Can you hear me now, Marco Polo?" A football field away, Lee leaned against the wall at the other end of the field, giggled and clearly heard what I had said. "Yes, I can!"

Sitting on a Chacmool, was like being in a London telephone booth. Chacmools were statues of reclining figures holding sacrificial vessels, with their heads turned to one side. To most archeologist, they are perceived as temple guardians. To us they were telephone booths. Sitting on a Chacmool, I cupped my hand over my mouth and talked to my sister a quarter mile away, as she sat on another Chacmool. "What are you going to do now? I have to change film on this camera." Without a care of how it happened or why, we played with the sound system of this immense sacred sight. I thought of her and our travels, "Can you hear me, Marco Polo?" I whispered to myself as I looked around the chamber here in up state New York.

Without a thought, my eyes glanced down at the owl wing and the ceremonial work we had done together. The owl and I had been working for several years on certain skills, only the owl could teach. Many people are afraid of the owl, because it is associated with the night, darkness, even death. In several North American native cultures, the owl is the night eagle. In the blackness of night, owls are rarely seen. They maneuver in silence, hearing everything with their sonar-like ears, which are offset. One opening is slightly higher than the other. This makes for a keen sense of hearing and audio detection. It is no wonder the Greek goddess Athena had an owl on her shoulder, who helped discern the truth. This beautifully sacrificed being was helping me develop my clairvoyance, not to listen to my internal chatter or to others, but to hear the voice of my Truth.

Facing East, I raised the left owl wing, with my left hand, into the air. Both of us were ready for flight. "Oh, Great Spirit, let this Being of Enlightenment, who sees through the deepest darkness, carry the Truth." I turned clockwise into the South and took a deep breath. "I honor, myself, my spirit and Creator. Let this Owl Being carry my family seven generations hence and seven generations forth into a new Springtime of health and prosperity. Let my family go from bondage of any kind." Bending down, I picked up the right wing in the other hand and swirled it into the westerly direction. For a moment, I lost my equilibrium. I heard myself chanting in another language. Part of me could not be a witness and participant at the same time.

"Druskis, pull yourself back. Don't go anywhere else. Stay in this reality!" A clear inner voice reiterated, "This reality." Lifting the right wing high into the air, I continued the prayer, "Fly westward to take physical form. Shatter the night. Pierce the veil between the worlds as the sun begins to set." Concentrating on breathing, the vowel "O" flew out of my mouth and landed in the chair that Running Horse had sat in. A sense of unexplained bitterness came over me. Tasting it, I spat it out with ugly disgust.

Looking Northeast, from the corner of my left eye, a full-blown picture of the North American Plains appeared. It was the dead of winter with snow drifts everywhere. Time froze like the landscape. Yet behind a huge snow embankment, I sensed a living Being. It was just born and this perplexed me. It had a big black nose and the steam of its breath was the only giveaway sign that it was there. Its fur blended in with the snow. It had four legs. A baby, lots of fur, slightly humped back. It was all too much to take in. I am not used to seeing events in picture form. That's a laugh, considering I was a professional photographer. Whatever vision I was witnessing; it was fixed in my mind, like a Kodak print that had just finished being developed, and needed to be hung, dried and reviewed under glass. The image didn't morph into anything else. Blinking into present time, I shivered.

I placed the left wing toward East and the right one toward West. In this configuration, the owl's head would have been facing South. The bird's flight pattern was directly from North to South. I looked down at the wings and whispered softly, "You will ride on the back of a buffalo in the coldest of winters. As both of you travel, quietly listen to the cold, hard truth. Then my friend, fly without a sound in the direction of the South to plant the seeds of wisdom. Together, we can watch them grow."

Several months later, the meaning of this vision would be revealed by a Native American friend, who called the house in Hoboken announcing that a White Buffalo calf had been born in the North.

Stepping out of the center of the Wheel, the Chamber preparations were finished. This regal chamber was created as a result of a vision Joseph, Beautiful Painted Arrow, had while Sun Dancing in 1983. He had seen World Peace Chambers around the planet, filled with people chanting for peace. For the past fifteen years, Joseph had dedicated his life to making this vision a reality. Now there were World Peace Chambers in: England, Norway, Australia, Germany, and several in North America.

To me, this Chamber was like the holographic deck of the good ship Enterprise; it was the New York City Hilton decorated for the Macy's Thanksgiving Parade; a Buddha field of a thousand lotus petals, and it was simply my good fortune to be in it here and now.

"Here," I said to myself, rather sheepishly, "What's going to happen in four days inside this huge Medicine Wheel. Let's see, Druskis, in Al-Anon, don't they say, 'Keep it simple. First things first.'"

I came to pray.

Praying is a ceremony. I decided to dress appropriately for this occasion. Marguerite, my youngest sister, made a powerful sweat lodge dress. I don't wear it often because it evokes strong emotional reactions in everyone who looks at it. The first time my friend Elizabeth saw it, we started to fight. "How could you wear that symbol? It's a Christian cross. The whole outfit... You look like a monk, let alone some Crusader from the 12th century." And to get my cultural "goat," she screamed, "What will the Native Americans think?"

The dress was flaming red. It had a hood, long sleeves and a wide skirt made of pure cotton. On the chest was sewn a huge cross. It has always amazed me what personal and cultural baggage we put into symbols. I wear this outfit when I am centered. I am not the symbol, the dress, the body or the mind. I am all this and much more. When I am grounded, I realize this ceremonial dress is a mirror in which others can view their feelings. But I am not their feelings.

In the Chamber, wearing my red sweat lodge dress, I put on a yellow jacket. The combination of colors reminds me of the Tibetan tradition.

As a little girl in my bedroom, I would recite these words with heart-felt delight.

Gate, Gate, Paragate, Parasamgate, Bodhi Svaha!
Gate, Gate, Paragate, Parasamgate, Bodhi Svaha!
Gate, Gate, Paragate, Parasamgate, Bodhi Svaha!

Twenty years later, four Tibetan monks in robes of yellow orange recited these same phrases. While listening to them, an instantaneous holographic past life twirled in front of my eyes. I was a little boy, four or five years of age, joyfully playing on the monastery grounds. I was adored and taken care of by all the monks. The temple grounds would exist forever, I thought. I had the childish feeling we were safe in this land for ever. The last holographic picture that entered my mind was of me as the same boy, now at age ten or twelve, dying from pneumonia. That boy, that me, could not be saved, even in this heavenly monastery and with a thousand monks praying: "Through my merit, may all those in all directions who are afflicted by bodily and mental sufferings obtain oceans of joy and contentment. As long as the cycle of existence lasts, may their happiness never decline. May the world attain the constant joy of the bodhisattvas." As that little boy, I felt betrayed. Why did I have to go? Couldn't I be saved by the Medicine Buddha? Was he not the greatest healer? Why? As I remembered these questions, the boy's body was eaten by vultures.

This vision explained my attraction and repulsion for the Tibetan tradition in this lifetime. Forgiveness has always been hard for me. Seven hundred years ago or yesterday, it is still challenging for me to process and forgive.

As my mind returned to the present, I started to make prayer bundles. Sitting in lotus position, facing North, I surveyed the tools needed: scissors, string, tobacco and four different colored cotton cloths. White, black, red and yellow. The cotton fabric cut into squares reminded me of the four directions. I started by picking up a piece of cut cloth and placed a pinch of tobacco inside it. Folding it into a ball, the bundle was placed next to my heart and prayers were said. During this round, the Medicine Wheel was specifically for my mother's family, seven generations back and seven generations into the future. In between prayers, my mind traveled to the Baltic Countries and to my mother who was Estonian, and my father who was Lithuanian. The male side of me identified with the great knights of Lithuania and the fact that Lithuania was the last pagan country in Europe. For some reason, I was proud of that. Mother Earth still ruled in the minds of men.

Over campfires, my uncle would regale us children with stories of Lithuania in the 14th century. This county did not have the same fate as the other Baltic Countries had during that time. The Latvians and Estonians were either converted or killed by German Teutonic Knights and Scandinavian colonizers. The Pope and European Christians called Lithuania "the Spawn of Satan." "All hail to Gediminas, the Grand Duke of Lithuania!" my Big Uncle would chortle into the blaze of the campfire. Because of Gediminas' foresight, diplomacy and lust for power, Lithuania would dramatically expand into land abandoned by the retreating Tartars and swarm all the way from the Baltic Sea to the Black Sea.

My mother's Estonia always seemed to be the underdog to some other country. Estonia never achieved political unity and became serfs by the 15th century. Their rulers included the Danes, Swedes, Germans and the Russians after the Second World War. Lithuanians may have worked the land, but they never owned it throughout 95% of their recorded history. This did not stop them from being one of the most intellectual countries in early Europe. The 1917 census reported that 93% of Estonian adults could read.

To me, the Estonian language is very lyrical. Their epic poem "Kalev-ipoeg," reminiscent of Virgil's "Aeneid," should be made into an opera. Listening to a group of Estonians speak, is to hear a forgotten species of exotic birds calling to one another.

My mind now back in the Chamber, I looked down at the tobacco bundles and placed them in the center of the Medicine Wheel. On each side of the large pile of prayer bundles were owl wings, as Guardians. With the air filled now with the aroma of tobacco, a sudden tiredness overtook me, filling me with satisfaction, as I prepared to embrace the dream world.

The next morning came quickly. There wasn't a need to answer to anyone, the ringing of the alarm, or the calling of some civilized time. It was me, awake and listening to birds fluttering as the sun's rays touched the big pines surrounding the Chamber. The roof was transformed into a major highway, as squirrels and chipmunks scurried about departing for their breakfast hunt. The Chamber and I were staying in place, not wandering off, but doing our best to be in the present.

The Chamber was a little damp, but I had been forewarned, so I brought clothing and sleeping gear ready for an Alaskan winter. I jumped out of my thermal-zero degrees, feather-lite sleeping bag and put on sweat pants under my ceremonial dress. Snuggly warm! Next, I searched for a Hope Garden Herb Bundle. My sister Marguerite had created these bundles of Cedar, Rose, Sage, Southern Wood and Thyme. She had taught me about the vibrations of these herbs. Cedar vibrated protection and strength. The warmth and vigor of summer are held in its evergreen branches. Its scent has been known to inspire divine thoughts. I could use some "divine inspiration," I mumbled, as I lit the bundle, and the familiar smell of sage filled my nostrils and purified the Medicine Wheel. The Southern wood comforted me, thanks to its ability to protect a space, while the Thyme enhanced one's clairvoyance. This girl needed all the help she could get in the area of receiving messages loud and clear. I faced the East and began my morning prayers of "welcoming the Sun," a ceremony Beautiful Painted Arrow did with us every morning during the Sun Moon Dance.

With the Chamber smelling sweet, fresh and purified, every direction was honored with prayer. The next order of business was to clear my mind, that meant two hours of meditating. My intention was to do it in half-hour increments. After ten years of meditating, my body knew thirty minutes of "time". The meditation started in the East and the body physically moved like the hand on a clock, every thirty minutes.

After sitting meditation came "walking Zen." In many religious traditions, walking is a spiritual practice. It was a bridge between sitting meditation and entry into everyday life. Mindful walking is a form of meditation in action. I started consciously being aware of my steps while walking around the Medicine Wheel.

I began to visualize the chamber and making meditation stations. Looking down into the chamber, each meditation station was a cardinal point of a square. When doing the "walking Zen," I created a circle around the square. This continuous dance of meditating and "walking Zen" had an altering effect on my perception of reality.

Very soon, the force field created by my physical movement and intention started to make the hair on my skin stand straight up, even my hair was getting uplifted. What would Michael Faraday think? He was the British scientist in the nineteenth century who conducted experiments in the field of electromagnetism. His most important contribution to physics was his development of the concept of a "field." He described a field as a magnetic and electric force. He coined the phrase "lines of force," which were fields of energy around every living Being. Faraday surmised that there was a force field between us. You couldn't see it, but it was there. He created a way of measuring the strength of these lines of force from magnetic and electrical currents.

In the Chamber, I was becoming aware of these electrical currents I had created by walking Zen. First, I felt the currents and seconds later, I could ride them. I was beginning to walk effortlessly. I was energy surfing; riding a Tesla car, if there would ever be such a thing. Folding the thumb of each hand into my palm and caressing the thumb with each finger of that thumb, the fingers created a cocoon for the thumb. Energy would not flow out of the body but recycle back into the body because of the thumbs position in the hand. I was becoming my own Tesla car.

This "riding on energy" reminded me of several Drum Dances in which I had used another technique to save energy. While at the Pennsylvania Drum Dance, the women would always sleep up on top of the hill over-looking the dance sight. Saturday night was a particularly hard evening for me and I usually dreaded climbing up the hill to my tent. By the fifth year of dancing, I had learned how to energy surf. At the end of the day, we women silently began to climb up the hill. I would find a dancer who had a high energy field and hitch a ride. That meant getting behind the person, synchronizing my step with theirs and locking into their energy field through the chakra system, upon reaching the top of the hill, I would break our link, smile at the person and thank her in my mind for the lift. This technique is used by good hunters and long-distance runners, when they run as a team.

"Wa Ma Chi," Joseph, would whisper as he was instructing me in his walking technique, on the streets of Manhattan. "Wa Ma Chi." Before his class he would always take a walk.

Seeing "ones self". How? The question floated to the top of my head. Joseph had written me a letter and asked the question: could I pass myself in walking Zen, then turn around and see myself. Joseph, always asked me to do things that would scare the shit out of me. I was too far inside the conventional box of life, until now. While walking, Joseph's letter kept appearing in my head. Could I pass myself, turn around and see myself?

Once when I was driving Joseph to a meeting, we talked about the American's love of cars, rather than developing techniques for time travel. Traveling through time rather than in a car, I began to consider this now and laughed. I was in good company, for apparently, Einstein, as a young boy, asked himself the simple question: "What would a beam of light look like if you could catch up with it? What was faster than light?" Joseph was inviting me to work with the vibrations of the fourth and fifth dimension. That is the realm Einstein wanted to leap into mathematically, the fourth and fifth dimension.

Now that my mind was on Einstein and numerology kept popping up. Why four directions? If East was one and it begot two in the South, how was two created? Two reminded me of the story of the "Twins" that Joseph used to tell during the winter when he would tell us wonderful stories in the cold winter time. Somehow the myth concerning the "Twins" will surface again in our culture and there will be a generation of women giving birth to twins.

At this point, my body could feel the field, but not enter into it. There is a difference between surfing the waves and becoming the wave.

Wandering thoughts, while in a body was not "walking Zen." I stumbled back into my body and was once again with the physical form, which activated a sense of hunger. Somewhere in the second day, a tinge of hunger finally entered my body. Time for lunch. Using a technique from the third year Drum Dance, I decided what to eat, greens and Evian water.

In 1988, I had danced two Drum Dances, the first in Malibu, California, and the second in New Mexico. It was in Malibu that Joseph taught us to drink with our eyes. He was giving the Drum Dancers words of melodious encouragement. Since I was hot, scared and associated only with my body, I heard nothing. There was no conceptual idea in my head how I was going to make it for three days in this heat, where 110 was cool in the shade. I looked around at the faces fixated on Joseph. I was fixated on fear. What broke the fear was the sound of a small bird chirping delightfully. She was playing in a nearby concert birdbath. I focused all my attention on the bird's activity of joyfully drinking from the fountain. The sound of her splashing in the water amplified in my ears. Turning my eyes to focus on the bird's movement, everything began to slow down. I was watching its activity the same way I read a photographic paper contact sheet. Frame one, bird bending over; frame two, bird scoops water into bill; frame three, bird lifts its head to swallow water. I was watching the event in animated time.

Suddenly, I slipped between the frame and then into the frame. "Down the rabbit hole, Alice. Down the rabbit hole." A distant voice echoed. With laser like awareness, I was the bird who drank the water and then became the water splashing against the rocks in the fountain.

Now in the Sound Chamber in Woodstock, it was my intent to recreate that process. I sat down and quieted my mind to enter that moment again and totally become refreshed. Laughing to myself, I got a better "picture" of how Jesus turned water into wine and everyone was fed. Next, I brought up the imagery of the green pine trees surrounding the Chamber. Breathing in the greenery, I was satisfied. The smell of the fur trees outside, feed me like a fresh salad. A vision of the water given to me after the first Drum Dance by Benito, made my mouth fill with moisture. Lunch was over.

An image of Sathya Sai Baba in an orange robe passed from left to right in front of my eyes, as the memory of his many manifestations and materializations unfolded in my mind. He smiled, lifted his hand and pointed in the direction of the East. Then he disappeared.

The day cycle flowed from making prayer bundles, to meditating in the four directions; playing the crystal bowls and walking Zen. Last was rest, before the cycle would start again. It was during playing the bowls that I had my first conscious out-of-body experience in the Chamber. The crystal bowls vibrated at the same rate as human bones. I could feel my bones vibrate as I played them. During Reiki sessions, when I played the bowls first and then started to work on a client's energetic system, they would quickly relax and become centered within their body. This was now starting to happen to me, I was relaxed enough to see my causal body around my physical form.

Sitting in the North, leaning over the crystal bowls, I circled its rim with the leather-covered copper rod. The vibration enveloped me like the aroma from a cauldron of cabbage soup. My whole body began to vibrate like Sally Perry did before she began channeling. When I pressed my lips together, even they were vibrating-tickling my tongue until my gums quivered like lunch-box Jell-O. Seconds later, an unexpected pop. The same popping when a button on my pants flew off after gaining five pounds.

Pop. I watched myself from above; blissfully playing the crystal bowls. In a colorful flash of saffron and red, the scene changed to a familiar Tibetan Monastery. There, an elderly monk played copper bowls that were placed near a sacred sand painting. I was there as a child monk. I loved to look at the White Tara mandala, "Om! Tara! Tu! Tara! Turey! Swaha!" She was the supreme guardian; the Bodhisattva of compassion. The White Tara was born in the tears that Amitabba shed just before he entered his nirvana and looked back at all of those he would leave behind. The smell of tree sap and tea with butter, the memories brought tears to my eyes.

Again, I remembered the lifetime of being a young boy in the monastery with pneumonia. I missed my playmates, yet, the monks loved us so. Why did I have to leave so early? As this vision played out in present time, familiar anger filled my lungs. "Why didn't they save me? I didn't want to leave." I began to sob into the crystal bowl. The infant inside longed for that home. This longing for refuge began to fester in my lungs in present time and I began to cough.

As I leaned into the bowl, a rich, mature male voice whispered, "The Tibetan Medical Tradition is yours to remember. See now the Green Tara, the Mother who is always ready to come to your rescue from the eight great terrors. You are fearless in the presence of this Divine Mother." I sat, tears streaming down my face, rocking from past to present. Exhausted, I staggered to my cot. Upon awakening, another layer of chatter was gone from inside my head. Swaddled in silence, my eyes took in the Chamber candles flickering in unison.

I heard myself ask, "What are you feeling, Druskis?" In my everyday world, feelings didn't matter much. You did what you had to do. Survive. What the body was feeling, the mind, the soul; there were no words to describe them. With no vocabulary for "feelings," there was no reference, no her/story, there was just no. As a little girl, it was frightening to sense that other people didn't feel the way I did. It scared me, knowing I would never know what was going on in my sisters' mind. To be different scared me right out of my body. I didn't realize that everyone of us was uniquely individualized upon birth. Since I was frightened of being "different," most of my life was spent constructing a world of "same" and shutting out what was the "other."

Now things were shifting. "Other" had its place. One begot two.

Enough shifting and realizations, I went to the cot, changed my woolly socks and fell headlong into sleep. As I drove into the underworld, the music from "Secret Agent Man," played in my head. James Bond in his red Ferrari and white dinner jacket leaned against the mahogany banister, which was to the left of the third-floor guest room of the Monte Carlo Casino. On the door to the guest room was the gold-plated placard, "Million Dollar Club- Guests Only."

James gave me a Money-Penny-come-hither-smile and whispered in my ear, "So, now I hear you are an agent of Reality. Hard Assignment."

My eyes shifted to see a tall Kiva ladder with Running Horse's hat hanging on the top. I woke up in complete visual recognition of the dream. "That was Running Horse's hat! I saw his hat!" I jerked myself up from the sleeping bag and started to write the dream down on a note pad. Like a school teacher trying to reach a dimwitted student, I kept reminding myself about Running Horse's hat.

Tiredness flooded my body and I fell back onto the cot. My rim state was lighter, which made for a clear conscious state of recollection in chapter two of the dream: Diana Rigg, "Secret Agent" girl, began to scream into my left ear, "Here, this will help you remember!" She handed me a pen. All at once, Sally Perry enters stage right in the dream.

She appeared in the parking lot of an exclusive golf course for women. It was a hot summer day and heat rose off the asphalt making her appear to be a mirage. Sally was wearing one of her elegant, flowing gowns, finished off with shimmering gold earrings. She began speaking very intensely about the "Introduction to The Keys of Enoch." She began to recite, "The keys for our human growth are both a spiritual and scientific understanding that must connect with each other. It's not one or the other. They are not separate." Sally shifts her body awkwardly, "I need to sit down." I spotted a black convertible T-Bird. I tried opening it, the door flung open. Both of us smile as we got into the car. She continued, "We are way past the question of existence and non-existence." She puts her forefinger to her lips, "How do I say this? "The Book of Enoch" talks about passing from one state of being to another. Reincarnation and more." She lets the word unfold very slowly. "Re-in-car-nation. Don't ask me what 'the ultraviolet spectrum and electromagnetic spectrum' have to do with cars. They talk about it in the book. But different forms of intelligence and how they can be used. Not cars. How do I say this?"

"That's right ladies! Get out of my father's car." A tall, conservative young man yelled.

I flushed with sincerity and responded, "We weren't going to harm your car. Don't worry! We just wanted a place to sit down and talk." I put my hands in the air. That said, we both got out of the T-Bird and began to leave.

Then the young, proud preppie sauntered over to his father. "No one is going to mess-up my father's car. Not here. Not now." But his father was clearly dismayed, shaking his head, and placed a loving arm around his son. Then the young man came over, holding his father's set of keys. "Here. My father wants you to have the car." I looked at him in astonishment. "Really!

He wants you to have the car." His attitude had shifted 180 degrees. "It's in good working condition. The clutch is a little sensitive."

With my mouth wide open and hands outstretched, I mumble, "Thank you." Came out of my mouth. Then the scene shifted.

Sally was hungry, "Really Laima, I don't care if you don't want to eat. I have to. Where can we go?"

Like dreams, time and space collapse in the mind and change instantly. We appeared in Santa Monica at the Interactive Café on Broadway. I looked around for familiar faces and nothing. A Hispanic waiter approached and took our order, while Sally spread her notes from the "Book of Enoch" on the booth table.

While Sally was drawing on her patience and compassion; I was distracted by a miniature man sitting in a baby high chair on wheels. He pushed himself off from the table and failed to grab the sacred book that was on our table. He tried several more times, never succeeding. "Pay him no mind!" Sally barked. I turned back to the large white pages with Hebrew symbols. They seemed to form dancing flames. All at once, my attention was captured by a mesmerizing letter. The intense focus shifted my perception.

In this dream scape, I am driving a black 1968 Volkswagen around Trafalgar Square. I stop for a red light, while huge drops of afternoon rain begin to bang against the hood of the car. Diana Rigg appears leaning against the hood. She is wearing this year's Armani fall cape that swirls around her left shoulder. Stretching her body further over the hood, she adjusts the windshield wiper. Cupping her leather gloved hands into a megaphone, she shouts, "Here! This will help your pacing and vision." It seems she is there to help not only my memory, but my sight as well.

"Damn that cramp!" My right leg jerks straight up and nearly flips me out of my sleeping bag. I grab it and furiously massage the back of my right calf.

On the third day, my body began to react to the lack of minerals and water. I was concerned about my kidneys working so hard, but the color of my urine was bright yellow, with no blood. Hunger pangs began to eat me for breakfast and a vision of the golden arches reminded me of some distant Mecca.

After dressing, I slowed down long enough to hear the birds outside and decided to use a Drum Dance trick to calm my galloping hunger. Sally and Ce Ce, came to mind. Ce Ce was an African American Mystic. She and Sally had worked with Joseph in different parts of the country and had danced this year at the Bissingers in Pennsylvania. As I remember them at the Pennsylvania dance; both of them walked in unison and kept to themselves. They carried their knowledge on their shoulders and in their hearts; their stride was long and purposeful. They had been to India together.

During the grueling second day of the dance, I watched Ce Ce's cool demeanor as she meditated during our rest periods. I was totally submerged in an ocean of hunger and couldn't figure out how she could be so calm. I learned later she practiced an Ayurvedic breathing techniques which helped her during the three-day fast. By closing her right nostril and breathing through her left nostril, her metabolism was slowed down. It was an old yoga trick to stave off hunger during the fast and helped balance the left and right hemispheres of the brain.

Here in the Woodstock chamber, I plugged up my right nostril with some toilet paper I found. Breathing through my left nostril allowed the image of the Golden Arches to melt away and the taste of a Big Mac to leave my mouth.

During my walking meditation, I became increasingly aware of how important movement was for perception and integration. While meditating in each direction, the physical activity of getting up and going to the next station gave me the impetus toward realization. Beautiful Painted

Arrow's phrase, "Wa Ma Chi," and his "How to Pamphlet on Walking" would speak to that concept. As I kept walking, a profound wealth of knowledge came to mind. I remembered Joseph talking about the power in the word walking. The word walking had three important letters: w-a-i. Walking woke up the neuro-muscular and circulatory system of the physical body.

.

While advancing to the next station, I whispered to myself, "Wa Ma Chi." A letter Beautiful Painted Arrow had written popped into my head. I loved it when he would draw something as an explanation of one of his lessons. In this letter, he drew the human body. He urged me to look at the energy that flowed up, down and across the human form. After meditating in the North, I got up and did something new. I walked directly to the South. I was beginning to understand something about energy flowing East/West and North/South. Now I took the image in my dream about Running Horse and superimposed it on top of Joseph's diagram of the body. I was getting very excited and started yelling, "Right. North where the inspiration and wisdom comes from; to be planted in the direction of the South, the emotional heart." Superimposing the two images, I thought of the similarity between BioGeometry and the human body's acupuncture system.

Somewhere in the human form is concealed the jewel of Enlightenment and movement was essential in discovering and cleansing this Lotus of Eternal Light.

Those Nike ads were right: JUST DO IT. The other half of the slogan is, "and enlightenment will come." I was gleeful, light headed, a Monopoly player on some kind of cosmic Boardwalk. "Go directly South and collect two hundred dollars." Twisting my body, trying not to step on some invisible crack on the floor, I began to skip like a school girl to the station of the west. "West, where I can watch my thoughts grow in physical form." Sally's dream symbols from the book: "The Keys of Enoch," danced past my left eye. The thought that ideas could take physical form, kept whirling in my head.

"I'm onto something!" I was ecstatic with delight, or was it just the light? Jumping up and down, up, up, down; my body catapulted headlong in an Easterly direction. Diving over the center of the Medicine Wheel, I tripped and fell.

The sound of rain woke me up that evening. Opening my eyes, I realized, I had fallen and was unconscious for some time. Lying on the floor, the realization came that part of me needed to get out of my body to go elsewhere. Awake and with my thoughts, I came to the conclusion that when working with the gross physical forms, the use of sound would break up the stuck particles in the body, faster than light. For this reason, using the crystal bowls would be an integral part of my healing work with clients and with integration with in myself.

Standing stiffly up, my arms touched the side of my legs. "Everything o.k., Doctor?" I asked myself. The answer came swiftly; the arthritic band in my lower sciatic region was making itself heard. "Not really, but it could have been worse," my body answered. I was stunned as the discomfort pinched and grabbed at my awareness.

It was time to meditate and begin breathing in the Heart Sutra, which gave me such solace as a child of ten. Now as an adult, conscious awareness guided me to softly whisper the sound of each comforting word, with more comprehension:

"Gate! Gate! Paragate! Parasamgate. Bodhi Svaha."
"Gate! Gate! Paragate! Parasamgate. Bodhi Svaha."
"Gate! Gate! Paragate! Parasamgate. Bodhi Svaha."

I breathed in on the "gate" and released slowly on the "Bodhi Svaha." A profound peace swept through me. Picking up the leather thong, I started to play the crystal bowl. The bones in my body surrendered to the crystal vibration. I didn't fight anything, any one or me. I just played while listening to the rain outside.

In a matter of minutes, the Medicine Wheel transformed into a three-dimensional holographic form. This is the way the Mayans viewed the Medicine Wheel. North and South were above and below. The human form was always placed in the center. Joseph's image appeared and then changed into Quetzalcoatl. The plumage on the flying serpent's headdress was dancing tracks of light which formed sacred geometric life forms in the air. In my mind's eye, these tracks of lights quickly created: triangles, stars, cubes and complex crystal patterns. I watched the pulsating lights appear and dance. The fall had knocked the sense out of me and I happily didn't need to know the "why" of anything. I watched the lights shift and play with the sound of the crystal bowl. This was magic. I was the Sorcerer's Apprentice in Disney's fantasy.

The thunderstorm outside the Chamber suddenly joined in the game, and soon we were playing a duet. The faster I would play, the sooner a crack of lightning would respond. Faster, faster. The copper rod twirled around the rim of the crystal bowl. The bowl became charged with a viscous feeling. This was power. I could feel the crystalline sound penetrate my bones. Electricity ran through me like Tesla rods.

And then it came in. The Fire.

It seemed to run from the electrical outlet along the wire to the ceiling lamp. I played; it crackled and danced. Then the smell of burning rubber put a stop to it all. I came to my senses.

"All right," I yelled. "You win, that's all I need!" I was furious with myself. "How am I going to tell Joseph that I burned down the Sound Chamber … let alone Betsy?!" Jumping up, I ran to the Chamber door and out to the Wittenberg Center house. A light brown coyote smirked came across my face. My body felt the water, glorious water all over my body for the first time in three days. Despite all the confusion, I was still thankful. Another part of me kept yelling, "Is anyone here? Help!"

Jim, who is part of the Wittenberg staff, stuck his head out of the attic porthole. "What's happening? We may be swimming here. Watch out!"

I cupped my hands into a megaphone and shouted to him, "You have to turn the electricity off to the Chamber! Right Now! There may be an electrical fire starting on the ceiling lamp. I can't unplug it. There's water all around the wall socket." Both of us took the stairs two at a time and swung the screen door open into the torrential downpour. Inside a small wood shed, Jim pulled the lever for all the electrical power.

"O.K. That should do it," he smiled. "How is it in there? You okay? We'll look at that line tomorrow."

All of my adrenalin was washed away. "It's not too bad. Just small puddles everywhere." My thoughts began to wander. "Water, water everywhere, but not a drop to drink.' Who wrote that?" The cot was wet. I was wet. My nagging thirst would not go away. The only thing left was to surrender to deep meditation. It allowed the feeling of water on my body to come into all parts of the inner me. Now the skin could taste the water, some gratitude was felt. But I realized, my ego would be served its glass of water sometime tomorrow.

The Chamber smelled of damp wool. The sounds from the dripping ceiling seemed out of sync. I shivered, wrapping myself in a garbage bag and once again cupped my hands into a megaphone, "Ladies and gentlemen, here at the Spring Gala in Monte Carlo, may I present to you this year's highlight: garbage bags! They come in Seattle White; New York City Blackout or Sun Valley Brown. Truly, a Drum Dancer's best friend. Ladies, on the East Coast it might keep you dry during that June thunderstorm. On the West Coast, it certainly will keep your body warm if dancing in high altitudes. No matter where you dance, it's plastic that will fill your needs!"

Cold and depressed, I stretched my legs the full length of the cot and stopped talking to myself. On the verge of a great discovery, I went too fast and lost it because of not being grounded. No patience. No balance. No memory. I sniffed my clothes and could sense some self-pity wrapped in mildew.

Most of the night I tossed and turned, trying to turn off the raging mind. Every part of me ached. I got up and moved the cot to a dryer corner in the Southwest. "You know, that part of the Wheel that has to do with the emotional-physical parts of me!" I said to myself, dryly. Around four a.m., something stirred and it wasn't me. Opening my left eye, peering directly at me was a drenched mouse. His teeth were chattering, sending Morse code for cheese.

"Come on, little one. Wish there was some cheese somewhere in here. I have a lot to learn about water." Joseph always said that abundance was represented by water. Abundance, what a concept for me. "I think there is some cornmeal up in the Northeast. I'll look for you, Mr. Mouse." Leaning my head on my shoulder, I surveyed the damage: some candles were out, but the large ones in the four directions burned brightly; the cardboard packing boxes for the crystal bowls needed to be dried out; owl wings were untouched by the rain. It seemed they had spent the evening tucked away in a magical nest, protected and wondering, "Who" should worry on a night like this?

The morning came; the real test of concentration was during my sunrise prayers. How could I sincerely focus on anything but my feet, when wearing squishy loafers. "My kingdom for a pair of dry socks!" I yelled toward the direction of the East, as I started the morning rounds of the directions. Joseph had taught us that all of life is a metaphor of some greater reality. This whole adventure started with Sally Perry seeing a foot stuck in my heart. I sat down and took off my shoes to look at my feet. They were wet, cold, and soggy. Maybe a first step toward becoming unstuck was to read the metaphor right. Water was abundance. Truth can sometimes be felt as a cold presence or cold Chi. Soggy could feel soft, which is usually associated with the feminine nature.

The metaphor for this situation seemed to be very straight forward: I needed to accept abundance into my life; look at some cold hard truths that were right under my foot and allow for the feminine side to open up more; which might take care of my constipation.

Still sitting, I closed my eyes to see if I remembered anything from the third night. A red neon sign flashed, "Use it or lose it." Opening my eyes, the first object I focused on was my medicine case given to me by Fred Wahpepah, elder of the Kickapoo and Sac-and-Fox tribes from the Seven Circle Foundation. Under my breath, I whispered, "I have to start doing sweat lodges and using the rattle of Sorrow and Forgiveness. That's it. Isn't it, Fred?"

The path was clear: I would fulfill my destiny by doing sweat lodges in which the heart could be opened through the endless cycles of acknowledging our human suffering and healing it with forgiveness. With that realization, it was over. I was done. It all seemed like a love affair that was finished: it was time to leave. I walked to the door and pulled back the tarp to let in the blinding, mind bending light.

CHAPTER NINE

"Finding One's Self"

Starting in 1987, I danced the Drum Dance for nine years straight. They were held in Pennsylvania, New Mexico, California, all over the United States. Each year something was growing and shifting inside of me. Each year, the dance would forecast the mood of the year. The obstacles on the dance floor were played out and most of the time resolved in the next twelve months.

The Sun-Moon Dances started in 1992. This dance was more complicated. That's how I explained it to my best friend Barbara. "The Sun-Moon Dance is a head-on collision with your greatest fears and yet, it's also pure bliss." I threw my hands up in the air in total frustration. Words were hard to wrap around this experience. Barbara in turn listened in utter disbelief, her hands cupped beneath her chin so her face, full of incomprehension, could be held upright. Barbara often held her face in her hands, as if it was a big chore that took an enormous amount of effort to ground such esoteric ideas in everyday life. Barbara had also learned that understanding such truths could be elusive. Running three businesses was a piece of cake for her compared to comprehending why her best friend did what she did. Yet, she was determined to understand, because something gnawed inside her, every time she thought of Joseph.

"Let me get this straight," she said. "You dance for three days without food or water and try to gather the courage to throw your body into a tree?" Now it was her turn to toss her hands toward the heavens in total frustration. The Santa Monica sunlight reflected off her amber colored Hollywood glasses. I leaned back on the patio chair, and for a moment, avoided going any deeper into why. So, I mentioned the roses that were planted around their aromatic Persian garden.

"How long ago did you and Rafigh plant those roses? They smell delightful. Are they...," I shifted my body to deflect Barbara's New York City attitude and Connecticut smirk.

"Screw the roses. Why are you doing this dance?" Barbara looked straight into my eyes.

I leaned back, closed my eyes and tried again to muster the thoughts that described this sacred dance. Like most native ceremonies I had experienced, this dance connected the spiritual, mental and physical aspects of myself in a very visceral way. Fasting without food and water allowed the body to purify, along with the mind. The spirit could easily rise up to other realms and perception depended on the individual's development.

I remember one evening Joseph saying the tree in the middle of the dance floor was made of "greatness." In his culture, wood carried the vibration of greatness. By hitting this beautiful tree, a dancer went past their fears into their greatness. By hitting the tree, the illusion of our physicality was made self-evident. When a dancer connected with the tree, sparks flew, as the lights were turned on in the psyche of their Higher Self. This connection helped a person go beyond the material form and their psyche was enlightened. A great awakening could be stirred within the gene pool of the dancer, when they hit the tree. This awakening allowed for ancient wisdom to rise up and true meaning of a dancer's existence could be revealed. That was one aspect of the dance that felt true for me. To have a vision of the "true self." A teenage smirk curled my lower lip, as I realized the irony of being a photographer and struggling with vision. I felt vulnerable sharing this with Barbara, even if our friendship went back thirty years. It was all about vision.

"It's about vision!" I blurted as I tilted the white enamel patio chair I was sitting in with my left foot. I needed some sort of leverage in this conversation. With the chair tilted slightly, my mind seemed clearer.

"Hmmmmmm. Am I hearing you correctly? Barbara replied. "As you would say, It's a sixth chakra thing. Odd. You being a professional photographer in Manhattan for some twenty years, yet now you want some vision. Dear God, have you gone mad?! There must be an easier way."

I touched my forehead and noticed sweat. My mind jumped to the class I had just finished teaching on chakras. I took a long breath and remembered saying, "Ajna is Hindi for the ability to receive without prejudice. It allows vast realms of light and darkness to open for a person's use. Some call it the 'Third Eye.' Inside the 6th chakra sits the third eye. This chakra deals with the gift of discernment for our beliefs and attitudes. Here is the witness, like a wise old owl who knew our false truths and encouraged us to listen for internal guidance. The way to open this chakra is through the guidance of a Guru, drugs or an extreme physical experience that forces energy through that chakra and cleans it for 'clearer vision'."

Covering my left ear with my hand, I tried to quiet the echo of Barbara's last rhetorical question. "Have you gone mad?" I twisted my body into a pretzel, as I realized the third eye also had a dark side to it. Most of the time we associate the third eye only with light. To have true vision, you need to see both the dark and the light side, just as in photography both are needed for contrast to make a good picture. The question echoed again, "Have you gone mad?" With my family history of depression and suicide, I wondered if I had gone mad? My father declared he was going to kill himself almost once a week until my mother looked him in the eye one morning and said, "Go, do what you must." From that day on, he never said a word again about taking his life. My sisters followed suit by trying to kill themselves, the youngest one in college. Life had other plans for them. As for me, I was always too busy with life to entertain the thought of suicide. But was I mad? To be honest, the world inside was not matching the outside and I was mad. Fucking angry to be exact.

So, I danced and Barbara was there for me; whether she like it or not.

Maybe dancing saved my life. In the Sun-Moon corral, I was safe to let out that anger because I trusted this ceremony and the people who lead it. We began the dance with the ceremony of feeding altars that had been placed in the four directions. Standing in the East, each dancer scooped their hand in a blue bowl filled with corn meal. It glowed in our hands. At this particular dance, Sai Baba's ash had been added. Walking clockwise, we stopped at each altar and made an offering of the cornmeal. Under each altar was placed a large garnet – the gem stone that could ground the body and connect to the present moment. I will always remember the feeling of the cornmeal trickling through my left hand as I bent over the altar.

That year, I had chosen the direction of the North as my dance spot. When we first walked into the corral, North was the direction I longed for. As we entered the sacred space, I thought of Benito, Joseph's brother. Benito was the one who gave me the accelerated learning curve on how to get the most out of the dance. "This is what you do: look at this scared corral with all the love you can muster. See and feel the spot that is the warmest - the spot you deeply desire. Then, turn around and go in the opposite direction." A huge smile crossed his face and with words that flowed like honey from his lips, Benito said, "What you know, won't teach ya'."

That's how I ended up in the South. The South was full of emotions and childhood memories hidden deep inside my sleeping bag. In this dance, I would learn what it meant to carry my ancestors. No pun intended, but I didn't know if I could bear it. That is how I ended up wearing a bear on my back at the dance. I was learning to consciously carry my ancestors.

Let's start again, with the beginning of the dance.

The dance never starts when you enter the dance corral, it starts the moment you make the commitment to dance. Mine was in Montana, three years ago, with Auntie Bear.

In all native cultures, animal totems have played an important role in personal development. All cultures believe animals have spirits and unique qualities. I have learned that there are spirit animals and animal totems. Spirit animals choose the person; animal totems are chosen by the person. Most of the time, our ego gets in the way and we pick animal totems reflecting our fantasies about gaining power or whatever animal is on the Disney top ten list for the year. When people choose their totem, they often become frustrated because what they truly need to learn is not innate to their imagined totem animal. It is always better to deeply understand the powers of the Mouse, than to be foiled by the glamour of the Mountain Lion.

It never occurred to me to have a totem. I was Laimute Elena Druskis. Laima was the Goddess of Destiny in the Lithuanian culture and Druskis meant salt of the earth. My Lithuanian name had deep meaning for me, as I was named after my father's sister Laima. That was enough. For fifteen years, working with Joseph, I had no desire to have a totem.

Then one early morning in Montana, getting ready to shoot a wedding, that all changed.

I sat up in bed, startling myself with these words, "Gotta get that bear." I opened one eye enough to focus on the alarm clock sitting on top of the hotel room dresser. "God it's only 5:30!" My other eye stayed shut knowing all along, it wasn't time to get up. After fussing about what to wear, I woke my friend Barbara. She stared at me from across the room with both eyes wide open. "It's early, what are you doing?"

"You won't believe this, I gotta get a bear." My eyes were in total disbelief, as the words came out of my mouth.

"Oh, no, no, no. You flew out here to shoot a wedding, dear. Not a bear. Remember! At 2:00 this afternoon, we are supposed to be at the Montana Country Club, shooting pictures of a very expensive, elegant wedding. Champagne! Caviar! Women in Vogue-like poses. Please say you remember!" Barbara cupped her right hand and once again plopped her face inside it. Looking at me from a horizontal position, she kept rolling her eyes around to see if that would help change the situation.

"No, it's ok. Really! I just have to find this bear. I'll be back in time to shoot the wedding. Trust me." Something inside me was very calm. My body seemed assured of every movement and with that, I jumped off the bed looking for clothes to wear. My psyche and body were fully informed as to where I was going. My ego and I just needed to follow my nose. I dashed out the door, not even looking to see if I had taken the local road map. The morning was full of wonderment, there wasn't any room for doubt.

I had been in this kind of state before. The name of the state was total trust. I headed the rental car North-by-Northwest. I smelled the mountain air using my expanded awareness and found the place within an hour.

The pure white sign with red letters painted on the mailbox read: Thomas Phifer/ licensed taxidermist. There were two log cabins at the end of the long driveway. Next to the smaller one was another white sign on the front lawn that read: Park Here.   It seemed very straight forward. It was 6:30 a.m. I figured someone had to be awake. Practicing my Girl Scout smile as I walked up the cobblestone driveway.

The face has forty-four moveable muscles that give us five thousand different expressions. As humans, we know the difference between a fake smile and a real one. When we make a sincere smile, the frontal cortex is stimulated and sends signals to the muscles, as fast as one sixteenth of a second. We can recognize that sincerity three hundred feet away, the length of a football field. I felt my lips begin to turn upward, as my eleven-year-old came into my mind's eye. I remembered standing straight and tall, knocking on neighborhood doors selling Girl Scout cookies. The feeling of success was coming to me in present time. The delight of knowing they would buy all of my boxes.

After several raps on the front screen porch door, Mrs. Phifer appeared in her shabby blue bathrobe. Or at least I thought it was Mrs. Phifer. Glaring through the screen door, her piercing words nearly hit me in the chest, "What do you want?"

"Good morning. You have a bear of mine." I decided to keep it simple, with this being so early in the morning.

"Thomas! Thomas there's a woman here that wants a bear." Her words were shrill, dripped with anger.

Mrs. Phifer had the high, piercing voice usually reserved for waitresses in any local dinners on route 66. I looked down, trying to avoid the volume of her frustration coming straight at me. "It's 6:30 in the morning, Thomas. Thomas, why in the hell did you make an appointment for this time?" Her voice trailed off, as I rounded the main house and saw the second small white sign with red letters: Thomas Phifer/ licensed taxidermist. It was posted next to the small cabin.

Looking inside from the front window, I saw her, draped over a chair. Just sitting there. My bear. I breathed a sigh of relief. Mission accomplished. Now my eyes swept around the room to take in the other animals: Lynx, raccoons, mallards, deer and a huge moose in the far Eastern corner of the room. On the mission oak desk sat an arrangement of stuffed humming-birds. I stared at the Mountain Lion, which looked like he was ready to pounce on his victim at any moment. Why not choose the Mountain Lion: kingly, sleek, full of courage? Why did I choose the bear? I don't like bears. First of all, they are too fat. I sucked in my cheeks, trying to make my face thinner. Bears can get really angry. I bared my teeth at the reflection in the window. Sighing, I had to admit that these were my qualities, too.

In the constellation Ursa Major, or "The Great Bear" in Latin, which contains the 7 bright stars that form "The Big Dipper" is the easiest constellation to recognize in the northern hemisphere. As a young girl, I'd go camping with our family and my father would tell us stories at night about the stars and the animals they formed.

Most reading material on totems, attach the power of introspection to the bear. I could imagine a big black bear finding a cave, ready to digest the year's experience. Sitting there all cozy, with a paw full of honey. The sweet honey would have reminded the bear of the truth gleaned from a winter's worth of meditation. Do bears meditate, I wondered? For several Native American Elders, I knew the bear's placement was in the West, deep in the intuitive right side of the brain. The she bear would place her cave within the pineal gland for spiritual awareness on the symbolic level. My teacher and friend Fred Wahpepah used to say the bear had a fine capacity for discernment. If the bear came into my dreams, Fred would fold his arms over his chest and say, "Well? How's your judgment? You wearing those rose-colored glasses again?" Then he would always laugh. My mind was still inside the sweat lodge with Fred listening to the rocks as the pipe was passed around.

"Lady, what do you want!" This wasn't a question, it was a growl with a question mark at the end. I turned my head to face the bearish man in front of me. I tilted my head backward to get a better look at him, since he was so darn close.

"Sorry, I was…," His beastliness took my breath away. "I was directed to come here. That's my bear inside." I poked my right index finger at the pane of glass.

Thomas rubbed his blazing red bearded chin and closed one eye to fix his gaze at the bear inside. "She came in yesterday. Did Danny Foster send you over?"

"No, but a friend of his did." I didn't know who in the hell Danny Foster was, but I always entered the sweat lodge saying in Lakota, "To all my relations," so, I figured Danny Foster had to be one of my relations. I paid

Thomas and listened to his instructions on finding a Bear Farm, owned by his second cousin Vinny. Vinny's bear farm was known far and wide. Thomas suggested I go there, since I was so interested in bears.

After placing the she-bear gently in the front seat of the rental car, I got into the driver's seat, leaned over, buckled up the bear first, and then myself.

"Now this is going to be interesting! Are you ready, because I'm going to need some support from you!" I said. Then I stopped breathing to listen if this bear would answer.

"Breathe, for God sake," I whispered to the bear, or was it to myself? One of us had to be in control.

I named her Auntie Bear and within the hour, we were heading North again to visit the only Bear Farm this side of Bear Paw Mountain, Montana. I had never heard of a bear farm, this side of anything. It seems that Danny Foster's cousin was Thomas' second cousin, who was related to Vinny and Vinny had the bear farm. If I sincerely wanted to learn about bears, Thomas said, as a bear expert, then I should visit the farm. After all, he added, it was so close.

"What good fortune, Laima," I said as I leaned over and whispered gently into Auntie Bear's ear: "Here we are at the right place at the right time."

No one could miss Vinny's bear farm. Every seven miles there was a red billboard in the shape of an arrow, pointing the way. TWO MORE MILES AHEAD: BEAR FARM. CAN YOU BEAR IT? ONE MORE MILE. And then we were there. I leaned over the steering wheel and squinted as I surveyed a dirt driveway extending past a two-story log cabin. A huge American flag was prominently displayed from a fifty-foot pole next to the front porch. Squinting harder, I saw a twenty-foot-high, barbed wire fence that started at the back of the house and went on as far as the eye could see. Behind the barbed wire fence, running alongside it, was a twenty-foot redwood fence. It all reminded me of photos of Auschwitz I'd remembered and I shuttered.

"Do you think we should do this?" staring wide-eyed at Auntie Bear.

A sign framed in redwood hung on the porch fence: Honk your horn and sign in HERE. NO EXCEPTIONS! I leaned over to the passenger's side and folded Auntie Bear, her nose leaning toward the floor of the passenger side. Hopefully, no one could see her that way.

"Maybe you should bend over a little lower. I'll do the talking."

I parked the car and did what I was told. After sounding the horn three times, Vinny himself, came side stepping out onto the porch. If Thomas Phifer looked like a bear, Vinny was a badger: short squinty eyes that peered out from under thick coke bottle glasses. His nose was long and seemed to wiggle as he sniffed the air in front of him for signs of trouble. He was pleased to have a customer visiting his bear farm. His smile revealed ground down teeth, stained from years of enjoying Black Mark Chewing Tobacco. It was a genuine smile and I flashed one back.

"Come to see the bears? It's ten dollars." He exaggerated the word ten. On this side of Montana, ten bucks could buy a lot. "Ten dollars and sign here."

"Sure." I was full of fear and excitement.

"Sign these papers," he said wiggling his nose. With his web-like hand, Vinny could hold a ball point pen and a clipboard easily. "It just says that me and my bears are not liable for mauling your car." He seemed offended by the fear that raced across my eyes, as he described the damage. Surely I understood, he said, that mauling was just a fact of life with bears.

"Hey, you go in there on your own and don't get out of the car. You hear me? Stay in the car. They won't hurt you or nothing. You gotta sign this."

His right index finger pointed to the yellow legal document. Then he walked toward the car and tried to stick his head in the driver's side window. Luckily, I jumped in front of him.

"You don't have any food in there? They'll smell that a mile away." He stepped back and let a sinister smile cross his face, which caused his nose to wiggle again.

I signed the papers. A small bead of watery fear trickled down my neck as I started the car and pulled slowly away, reciting prayers to Lord Ganish for our protection.

This was the first zoo I ever visited where the people were in cages and the animals roamed around seemingly free. Driving at a snail's space, the branches of huge conifers bowed down to inspect our intention, as we drove by. The shadow of the branches cast a dubious feeling inside me. I cleared my throat. With my left hand gripping the steering wheel for dear life; my right arm extended out and around Auntie Bear's neck, "Sit up Auntie Bear. You're not scared, are ya'?"

The road had become gravel and I did not deviate one inch from it until the thud. The shift in the car came from the rear right side. One should never try to share a single lane road with a five-hundred-pound brown bear. He or was it she, always has the right of way. Eyes wide open, mouth wide open, foot on brake. Breathe in, breathe out, that's all I could do. He was the biggest brown bear I had ever seen. He was as big as the car, maybe bigger.

The Alaskan brown bear is the largest flesh-eating animal in the world. They can weigh as much as fifteen hundred pounds. These bears mind their own business but will protect their young with great ferocity. When angered, they can run at the speed of sixty miles an hour. This one was not protecting anything; he was just curious. He was in the mood to saunter up to the car and take a look-see at that beauty sitting next to me.

Information about bears seemed to flood my brain, as if that might help keep my sanity: countries as far apart as Finland, Siberia and Japan consider the bear to be a sacred animal. They are known as "Masters" who teach the human shaman their skills. In the Finish Kalevala, the bear is respectfully called the Great Fur-adorned Master. In the Kalevala, after the killing of a bear, a great feast was had; most of the feast was filled with songs and stories convincing the bear's spirit that his body was accidently killed, never murdered. In keeping with tradition, the bear's skull is hung atop a pine tree so its spirit can travel into the heavens and reenter another bear, during the winter. My mother had those amazing tapes of the Estonian bear festival. What did they sing? Pictures of Japan floated across my eyes; the bear represented benevolence and wisdom for these people. This is time to be brave, Laima. Be a Viking! We could use some of those psychotropic mushrooms the Vikings would eat to work themselves into frenzy while invoking the bear spirit.

The ghost of Michael White Feather crossed my mind, as he whispered into my ear, "I tell ya', girl, I shot a bear, skinned him and never went hunting again. After skinning it, that there bear's body reminded me of myself. That skinned devil looked sooo human. It was all too close, if you know what I mean. Nope, never again." I could feel his breath from another dimension.

"Auntie Bear do you know that big guy outside?" I was the caged animal in a foreign land. Gingerly, I pressed down on the gas pedal and drove on. The big brown bear sniffed the air, turned, and walking in the opposite direction. "Thank God he didn't remember you!" For another hour we witnessed a wonderland of bear activity, too intimate and familiar to share.

When I got back to the hotel, there was just enough time to check the battery packs and make sure I had an extra camera body. That night:

Thomas Phifer, the farm, the wedding all seemed surreal to me. As for Barbara, she kept going back and forth from her bed to the hotel room closet to look at Auntie Bear and kept whispering, "Don't ask. Don't tell."

Arriving home to my beloved Ojai, I put Auntie Bear to sleep for the longest while. She came out of hibernation in my imagination one Tuesday morning on a Delta flight to New York City. I had a photography assignment in Manhattan. I've always considered airplane flights, premium office time. Strapped into the seat, you are forced to stay with what you've got: unanswered mail, books that should have been read a month ago, schedules for the shoots on yellow legal pads, with the words: "call the crew" in orange ink. I was lucky enough to have no one sit next to me. On that empty seat lay the sketchbook full of bearish thoughts and drawings. "What shall I draw on the skin?" I closed my eyes and nothing seemed to appear. Then Michael White Feather's thoughts came back to me, "That skinned devil was so human like." I needed to draw the energy system on her. That's what I needed to do for Auntie Bear. Chakras first. With pen in hand, I drew the swirling balls of energy. The womb was a cave with paw prints all around. Since I worked with crystals, they would be her teeth. Turquoise stones were her eyes. Next came her paws, I leaned back in the seat and unbuckled my safety belt to stretch. I put out my right hand and stared at it. What was it like to have a paw, as big as the Ursa Major? I closed my eyes to see the stars in the evening sky and how they would be painted onto each paw. Totally relaxed, around the corner of my eyelid, a video started to flicker.

The year 1912. The country Estonia. The weather bitter cold. The women were dressed in traditional costumes. The men wore bearskins over their shoulders. They were in a log cabin feasting, singing to a gigantic stuffed bear seated at the front of a long table filled with blood sausage, sauerkraut, Rosolje, black bread, Sult, pickled yellow pumpkin and ale from birch or beer hops. The anticipation of Spring seemed so sweet to this group of Estonians.

My mother only spoke once of the Estonian Bear Society. This society had the job of keeping up the grave yards, caring for the dead and dying. For the people, it was a miracle that the bear went into its cave at the beginning of winter and came out alive the next spring, sometimes with young. That is why this Society revered the bear. It was through his or her spirit that the people would learn how Shaman Bear came alive again "It is all a great Mystery," she would whisper on her deathbed.

I spent two years crafting my bear suit. Now on this New Mexico Sun Moon Dance floor, we were going to be born again.

The first morning of the Sun Moon Dance, I put on a black t-shirt and cotton running pants. Then I smeared my face with earth red pipe stone shavings Rick had given me many years ago. Since I didn't carry a pipe anymore, this act reminded me of becoming the hollow stem, that connected with the pipe bowl. This connection symbolized the joining of the male and the female aspects of an individual. It also represented the act of men and women joining in sacred union. Then I draped Auntie Bear onto my shoulders. Her head sat squarely on top of mine. A black belt was sewn around the waist, the belt allowed the weight of the bear to be carried by my hips.

It was custom in this dance for all of us to do a morning ritual of covering ourselves with a white sheet, walking outside of the corral and singing a sunrise song, that Joseph taught us. We watched the first rays of golden light dart across the horizon. It was rather odd seeing this Black Bear covered with a white linen sheet, standing next to all the dancers. Many years later, one of the dancers, who stood behind me that morning, told me he thought he was hallucinating, while looking down seeing such hairy legs of the dancer in front of him, "God," he thought, but his mind couldn't hold the contradictions, "What an animal! What's happening?"

I was proud of my bear, she was a comfort in two very strange ways. The temperature was extremely hot in the desert this year. Wearing this bear suit, acted as insulation. My sweat couldn't evaporate so quickly. I stayed cool. Secondly, Auntie Bear was my protector from watchful eyes. I didn't realize how vulnerable I felt until I took the bear skin off and started dancing in my buckskin dress. Auntie Bear was my guardian against all those observing with critical eyes; least I expose the image I held dearly of myself. It is odd how the personality can play tricks, wanting desperately not to change in any way shape or form.

After the sunrise ceremony, we would go back into the corral and wait until the drum called us. It was a huge drum. Four drummers could easily sit around it. The skin of the drum was buffalo and it was truly a singer. Benito and his daughter, Karla Jo were the two main drummers at this dance. When they sang to each other across the drum, they were lovers calling to their ancestors across time and space. They sang to each dancer's longing for a vision. Each vowel out of their mouths kissed the air and thanked each one of us for coming to work so hard. As Joseph would remind us, "Work is worship."

By mid morning, the scorching shafts of light cut through the air and sizzled as they pierced our skin. The sun was already asking for an offering. Joseph had told me to keep a stone in my mouth, it would hold the moisture. I was afraid of swallowing it. So, I kept licking my lips, that were ever searching for a drop of moisture.

The blue traps covered part of the corral. There we laid down between dances and slept. It gave us shade, keeping the temperature a cool 110 degrees Fahrenheit. Someone said it was seven a.m., a lifetime would pass before noon. The phrase, "Only mad dogs and Englishmen go out in the noonday sun" kept running through my head, as I looked around the corral at my fellow dancers. During this break, I put Auntie Bear on the floor, next to my sleeping bag. I was wise enough to keep her off my back, until the thunder of the drum.

And it did come.

The drum skin was tight. Its vibration came as a high pitched "theeee-udd" sound. We all stood up ready to dance. For me the excitement had left with the sunrise song. Sweat trickled down the sides of my back to join Auntie Bear's skin. We shared much that could not be seen during this dance. By focusing my mind on the tree, I drew strength from it. In my mind's eye, it was the opening to Babaji's cave. I had seen pictures of that cave when reading about India. In a vision, my mother placed her hand in my left one, and with my right palm open, my father placed his hand in it. I made a fist to feel their presence, past the veil of their deaths. I hadn't realized how important family was until the death of my parents. So, it was exactly right to be in the direction of the South, in search of my inner child and family.

The heat and lack of water started drawing out all my fears from my first chakra. The operating words for the first chakra are: "survival" and "identity." This chakra loves drama. It deals with events that are life-altering: picking a partner, changing jobs, life-threatening illnesses. When someone wants to shift any of the above events in their life, they may feel like they are going to die, because they are dealing with perceived survival issues. Surviving deals with the physical body. One of the ways to stimulate change in the first chakra is through sex. That is why some people who are dealing with identity issues will have many intense sexual affairs. They need that stimulation in order to shift the first chakra. Few people know of Tantric stimulation to shift this chakra that does not include a sexual partner. Having a child will also change how you view and change the survival/identity chakra. I have observed that when people have "accidents," there is some sort of conflict with their first chakra. When people change certain parts of their identity, the body may feel like it is being killed and panic attacks are a first chakra symptom during this development of identity or changing of it.

By one o'clock the sun was unbearable. As Sun Moon Chief, Joseph decided to grace us with stopping the dance for a few hours. We went back to the corral, to shade our painful bodies. I didn't know which was hardest, the sweltering sun or sitting in the shade with my "identity."

An odd fear had arisen in the past hour. Lying on my sleeping bag, I realized a reoccurring dream. It was here again to taunt me. I would wake up from a dream unable to take the bear suit off. I had become the bear. Our faces had melted into one. I would panic in the dream, trying to tear the bear off my body. On the sleeping bag, I turned over to look at the bear skin next to me. I whispered to her, "Who am I?" Pictures of my mother and father blurred my vision. We certainly were not the typical American family. How my mother longed to fit in. When my father would sternly look down at his three girls and say, "You do it because I'm your father!" he was speaking from his first chakra. He had a clause in his first chakra contract, "in order for me to be a successful parent, I have to raise my girls to be mothers and one of them will be smart enough to be a doctor!" We had a long line of doctors in our family.

The first gift I can ever remember under the Christmas tree was a small doctor's bag with my name of it. The family expectations were huge. My aunt was a doctor for the Lithuanian community in Chicago; one of the first women doctors in that community. Our family would drive to Chicago to visit on the weekends. I remember sleeping in her bed one Saturday night and being woken by the shill ring of the telephone. It was the hospital calling about one of her patients. I will never forget my Aunt yelling into the phone, "My patients don't die!" I carried that moment for many years, knowing the responsibility that your patients couldn't, wouldn't, shouldn't die. It was too big of a responsibility and anyway at seven, who could figure out what kept people alive.

The sounding of the drum brought me back onto the dance floor and the feeling of dryness covered my body. The heat began to melt the layers of auric fields around my physical form, creating unbearable discomfort and frustration. I had not met a teacher that might point the way to separation between church and state; the body and the soul.

My bear and I were one, with little perspective and no compassion. Now as the heat of the day engulfed me; suiting up was hard and Auntie Bear was a burden, not a blessing.

I wanted to get it over with. "Just run and hit the damn tree." I stood up and ran head on toward the tree, but stopped just short of hitting it. Fear, like the desert heat, buffeted us from the last step. There was a wall around the tree that I couldn't penetrate. It didn't allow me to hit the mark. Just finish my job and go home. I hadn't learned yet that inner awareness could signal the right moment in which the body, mind and spirit could galvanize the Being into action, cutting through any fear. So, I kept trying instead of just dancing. The energy for accomplishing my goal, required a tremendous effort by my soul as my ego fought its own battles.

My self - identity was invested in the first scenario; I was going to make this dance happen. "Mad dogs and Englishmen, go out in the noonday sun. Mad dogs and…." My trisynaptic circuitry had developed an earworm, as I ran back and forth, back and forth, to the tree, stop, back and forth. "God, when is it over…mad dogs go out in the noonday sun. God…" I was developing melodymania, until Joseph came over, carrying his eagle wing in his right hand. He walked to the right side of me, stepped into alignment of my stride, leaned in and whispered in my ear, "You don't have to carry a whole nation." I was startled by his words and his physical presence shifted my auric body.

In the beginning of our relationship, I hated when he did that to me, shifting my aura. I didn't know what was happening to my body. The first time he did that, it seemed like such a small incident. Joseph was leading a sweat lodge at the Bissingers. A large number of people came to attend and this sweat was fiercely hot. Joseph came out of the lodge and gently brushed my shoulder. To the untrained eye, it was just a gesture of the hand brushing up against someone in passing. For those with extended sight, you could see how he brought the auric egg surrounding my body back into alignment. For the quickest moment, I was in a revolving door, twirling and then stepping back into this earthly realm. Body awareness was not my forte and anger was my first response to that lack of perception of body and aura awareness.

The second time he shifted my envelope was during a Drum Dance. I had gotten myself into a real rut, dancing back and forth, back and forth. Fear was all I knew. In this particular dance, we had to dance to a line of feathers; stop, then dance backwards to the place where each dancer started from. I had the greatest fear of falling backward and hitting my head on the ground. So, I focused my full intention on each step. All sound was blocked, there was no one on the dance floor except me, I was going to dance forever. I was never going to fall.

With that thought, a shadow crept up next to me, then a form, it was Joseph. My body prickled and then nothing but pure honeydew bliss came over me. White light covered my eyes and that's all I remembered. Lying in a fetal position on my sleeping bag, I awoke with a huge grin on my face.

"Wooweeee. That was somethin' else watching you out on that dance floor. Did you hear us cheering you on? Man, he really hit you hard with that wing. Did it hurt? Hmmm. Hmmmm?" Two of the male dog soldiers bent over me and created shade for my face to show complete astonishment.

"Hurt? Nothing. I felt nothing." I smiled and twisted my head left, then right. The realization hadn't hit me that the cheering I had heard earlier, came from the dancers wanting me to fall and end the dance. I was the last dancer standing. I hadn't heard Joseph give the instructions that we would dance until everyone was down. They wanted me to get on and finish the dance. All I wanted was to keep dancing, never to fall. Energetically, the path my feet had made dancing back and forth to the feathers became my lifeline. I thought it was my life, not a line of energy.

Now, at this Sun Moon dance in New Mexico, I never felt the wing.

Upon reflection, when consumed by the light; the body totally relaxes, and the mind goes into a state of bliss. Joseph's action of blessing me with the Eagle wing broke the cycle in my head and shifted my body.

His words came back to me, "You don't have to carry a whole nation." I remember how he rolled the word "whole" inside his mouth and his cheeks puffed out for a moment, before the word came out, wrapping me in concern. His caring allowed me to stop dancing and be in the white light, without falling. My shoulders slumped as I regained my vision. Turning away from the sacred tree, I walked back to my space and my sleeping bag. The bear was wet with perspiration and that made me smile. Druskis, salt of the earth in dear Lithuanian. How remarkable that the bear and I should share so much. I placed the bear on the ground to rest and laid my body on the sleeping bag, hoping to do the same.

"You don't have to carry a whole nation" echoed in my ears as I breathed in the vowel "U". Joseph said the vowel sound of "u" was about carrying. I wiped my face on the sleeping bag. It smelled of perspiration and desert wind.

"We are all carrying something; women carry babies, boys carry guns and dogs sit in the noonday sun." Like a dog, I rolled over on my side, trying to find some sort of comfort in this hellish heat. My mind tried to get back to carrying and how Joseph had related it to the Medicine Wheel; "The vowel "U" is the center of the Medicine Wheel and when we go around the four directions, then we are ready to be carried to the next level of awareness," Joseph said. "God was carrying all of life as ideas that are constantly appearing as insights." I laughed at the word insight. We were God's insights. I closed my eyes and had the image of the word "insight" as being a light pictograph that became a geometric form full of color. This geometric form was our bodies. Joseph poetically described humans as "medicine bags."

"A medicine bag contains certain articles deemed sacred and holy by the person to whom the bag belonged. We humans carry 'Holy objects?' in our psyche, the medicine bag. These Holy objects are holographic forms of dancing light that play within our DNA and RNA." For now, the only dancing light I could carry was the feeling of heat, in and around my body, which was lying on a sleeping bag, in a corral under the noonday sun.

Joseph reminded us that this dance ceremony would teach us the ability to carry our physical form through fatigue and not have our problems suck up our energy. The key to this discipline, was in the Tiwa word "Tsclo-li-eh," which means, "One is at rest." To not get tired, one had to balance three energies. Joseph described these energies as: descending light that was coming into the dance, the creation of childlike innocence within our consciousness to receive the light and awareness that would recognize the other two energies.

All of his words meant nothing under this wretched, drying heat. I had become a mad dog, panting, with crusty salt-tasting chapped lips that could still create foam on the edges of my mouth. "Fuck the bear. Fuck the dance!" I spat the words out and growled. This mad dog was trying desperately to run away from the all-encompassing Light.

My mind was saved by the drum calling us to stand and dance to the tree. My legs were like Jell-o. Looking down at the bear, I had no compassion for her or me. "Fuck you." I turned away, unable to carry her any more. I abandoned her by turning away. I looked at my deerskin dress wrapped in Lithuanian linen on the other side of the sleeping bag. Maybe the dress was just another form of Auntie Bear. Falling to my knees, gasping for air; I unrolled the linen cloth to reveal the deerskin dance dress. I had tucked it into my sleeping bag when I packed for the dance. It was simple, light and feminine. I did not know if I could make the shift. The dress had fringes on the arms and simple red-white-blue bead work laced the neck and hem. Would it matter if people could see my mad dog, the feminine, the Light?

Surrendering to the sound of the drum, there was no discomfort, no thinking, no insights. The vibration of the buffalo skin broke the neural circuitry that was built up in my auditory cortex. I got up and took my place in the other dancers.

This time when the drum sounded, it carried me straight to the tree-unabashedly forward, without a thought. My body in motion made a direct connection with the tree. Finally, I hit it. I ran through the wall of fear and hit the tree as hard as I could. Then all was gone: the dog, the bear, the noonday sun.

I had the most blissful vision of my mother, father and me sitting in Babaji's cave, before consumed by white light.

CHAPTER TEN

"Fly Brave"

"Coke? Something to drink?" The stewardess asked. Her words snapped me back into the Delta 737. Her blue United uniform vest accentuated her large breasts. The smell of Chanel Number 5 filled my nostrils, as she leaned over the empty seat to take my order. I gasped, realizing where I was, "Yes, a coke with very little ice." I shivered, both realms were cold. The sugar and caffeine jolted my body and my personality was back in the plane flying toward Sacramento. My psyche had been idling too long between worlds after the dance. My body shifted uncomfortably in the small confines of the airplane seat, as I closed my eyes to breathe in the questions that surrounded me after the dance. How would this Sun Moon Dance relate to my family in the future? Where was Babaji's cave? Who was waiting in India? Why India?

"When the information is needed, it will appear." Joseph's words crept into my left ear, as I blew out a huge sigh of relief. Awareness and timing were the handmaidens of all grounded information.

"We would like to take this time to thank you for flying United. Please remain seated until the airplane stops. Welcome to Sacramento, where the time is 7 p.m." Auntie Bear and I were coming home to Davis. So much had happened at that dance. The steward's voice trailed off, as all the passengers focused on their personal belongings and their minds rushed to the baggage claim.

CHAPTER ELEVEN

"The Healing House"

Davis is thirty miles from the Sacramento airport, a university town that's liberal to the sixth degree-which means, a person can make at least a small shift in any direction and not be out of the box covered with the veneer of liberalism.

Tenth Street is just off "F" Street. That put my house within walking distance of the center of town. I was fortunate enough to have an office in a little granny flat behind the house. The granny flat is where I started my practice as an energetic healer.

On the East Coast, I had become a Reiki Master and on the West Coast, I gathered more tools to help activate the healing process within myself and my clients. These tools I began to gather were: the use of flower essences from Australia, aroma therapy, sound therapy using the crystal bowls and Reiki.

The use of sound and its healing qualities was introduced to me by Joseph. Joseph's book, Being & Vibration, lays out a foundation for under-standing vibration. In addition, all the hours I spent studying with him in Manhattan gave me an inkling of the field called vibration. As a result, I chose crystal bowls as my venue for creating sound therapy within my practice.

The work of Ian White from Australia provided me with the Bush Flower Essences. I will always be in debt to the Aboriginal who appeared to me twice to introduce the Australian Flower Essences. The first time he appeared was on a balmy Spring day while driving along the Pacific Coast Highway One, right outside Malibu. The egg white stratus and cumulus clouds were hovering over the Pacific Ocean. Driving on Highway One always made me anxious, but the beauty of the sky and ocean helped to calm me. Coming around a bend, I noticed a black man standing by the side of the road. The color of his skin was ebony and it glowed. He was wearing a white shirt, black pants and was waving at me. I slowed the car to a turtle pace, then stopped so I could observe him in more detail. I inspected him the same way I used to check out a prospective customer before opening the door of my cab, when I drove one in Manhattan. Your survival depended on how well you could size up a person when you drive a Yellow Cab for a living. No one got into mine unless I felt okay about them. This man was sweating profusely; his shirt collar was wet and dark red soil had created an ebony ring around his shirt collar. No jewelry, no watch. His salt and pepper hair was curly and wild. His jet-black eyes were pleading for something, but I didn't know what. He wore no shoes. In his left hand, palm up, was a cluster of tubular yellow flowers. The lobes on the flowers were rolled back and their stamens were jutting out. With his right hand, he made the universal sign for stop. I became instantly irritated when I looked into his eyes in the same way I became irritated when I first met Joseph in Park Slope, Brooklyn. I would soon learn he was an Australian shaman from the Kakadu tribe. Light bent and shifted around him.

"No, no, no! Not this time. I can't do this again," I said to myself. I gunned the engine, which made the Camry jump to sixty in a heartbeat. I could no longer see him in my rear-view mirror as I rounded the second bend. My heart stopped racing along with the car. I had escaped, and he was gone, never to be seen again.

Out of sight, out of mind until that Sun Moon Dance in Texas.

So there I was in Texas at the Sun Moon Dance, ready to die after the second day. I was getting too old for this. With thoughts like that, my mind could spin for days. Then it happened, I surrendered. I gave up. The ego was so tired, the chatter stopped and for a few moments, the mind was still and I was present. But present to what? This Texas soil was red, and the sky was full of gallon size tufts of cumulus clouds. Texas is big, wide and full of grandeur. That year, it had been a rather wet spring and the countryside was filled with the show of forty cactus species that produced very large, garish flowers in shades of yellow, red orange, pink and magenta. The desert sage was exploding with blossoms of pale lavender and deep purple.

All at once, the sun seemed brighter, sharper as I danced. Shielding my face with my left hand, my eyes looked down to gaze upon a cluster of yellow tubular flowers. They reminded me of something. My right hand involuntarily made the universal sign for stop. At that same moment, the Kakadu Shaman's face appeared as an overlay on the flowers. The same pleading, penetrating, jet black aboriginal eyes looked deeply into mine. This time I knew he was from Down Under, coming up to give me some information about flowers. I smiled, he smiled. It was worth the whole suffering, hot, forever-frigging Sun Moon dance, to get that connection. From that moment on, I started specializing in using the Australian Bush Flower Essences in my practice. That connection resonated deep within my soul. The Australian Bush Flower Essences would be part of my healing repertoire.

If the flower essences were to be ingested and quickly affect the chemistry of the body, then aroma therapy would affect the largest organ of the human body: the skin. With aroma therapy, the sense of smell can stimulate the limbic system of the brain and affect the central nervous system. I chose the Young Living Products. They were developed by Gary and Mary Young of Utah. They have been proven to create the best and most authentic essential oils in the world.

For basic detoxing during a healing process, I always suggest a sweat lodge, but the more traditional clients preferred an Ion Cleanse. The procedure for an Ion Cleanse is placing your feet in a tub of water, in which an electrode system is placed. This machine converts AC electricity to low power DC electricity. The electricity and the metal inside the machinery split the water molecules into $H+$ and $OH-$ ions. These ions travel throughout the body, neutralizing certain harmful particles. Through a powerful osmotic pressure, created by the Ion machine, it pulls out those neutralized particles from the body into the water.

For smokers and people who work around harmful chemicals, the first order of healing is to rid their bodies of harmful toxins. Seventy percent of my clients wanted and needed to detox their bodies and chose Ion Cleanse, plus the foot rub afterwards.

I was one of seventy percent who needed detoxing my body. For twenty years, I worked in a small lab developing pictures, at least two days a week. Who needed rubber gloves to develop, stop and fix black and white photographic prints? Not I! The sweat lodge and then the use of the Ion Cleanse saved my life. First time I came out of a lodge, green puss poured out of my eyes; I couldn't see, let alone drive home after the ceremony. The lodge started the physical purification process for me; the dances addressed my psychological problems and deep-rooted past life spiritual needs.

Now it was my turn to give back for all the healing work that had been given to me through my healing practice. My healing office was luxurious. The entry led into a room that was large enough for a massage table and comfortable lounge chair for me. In the southeast corner sat the crystal bowls which were gate keepers ready to connect with a client's bone frequency when played. The bathroom was small but stylishly decorated in Moroccan tan and avocado green. The room had two large windows; one of them looking out onto a swimming pool.

The only item in the room that reminded anyone of an office was the black metal, seven drawer filing cabinet. Inside it, I had arranged my clients' files by chakras. Seven main chakras in the human body, seven drawers, it was perfect. Ninety percent of my clients had a predominate chakra problem and that is how I arranged their data intake.

The chakras are pathways forming vortexes or terminals within our energetic field that surround our body and influence all of our internal organs. In the Western tradition, we call the substance that rides in this system bioenergy. How bioenergy interacts within our body and our surrounding environment, determines our health and vitality.

My office was open by appointment only. Before a client came, I would review their file and then sit down to meditate. Quieting my mind was paramount to listening. Not just listening, but listening with conscious awareness. Conscious awareness demanded a non-judgmental witness. Most of us have an agenda that sits upon a well-developed ego. My ego needed to "fix it." My aunt was a well known doctor in Chicago. She was my elder in the healing practice. My primary care doctor in Sacramento needed to protect his practice from lawsuits and prescribed antibiotics for almost everything, except foot fungus. My aunt, my doctor in Sacramento and I; we all wore rose colored glasses. The question was how could we take them off to hear the true needs and see the healing potential of our clients?

Standing next to the file cabinet with those thoughts, I kicked the bottom drawer muttering, "Come on, Clyde. You aren't gonna die." For sure he was the classic first chakra client. He had come to the office with a full-blown panic attack. He was a drama queen. "I'm going to die!" So, we needed to work on his first chakra if he was going to recover from this illusion.

The first chakra represents life and death; our basic identity resides there. There our sexual feelings are programmed from the last life time and tested or enhanced by the family we are brought into. Here is where traditions are kept.

Clyde was a fine example of a first Chakra dilemma. At eight years old, Clyde had wanted catfish for Thanksgiving, not turkey; at twenty-three, he wanted to bring home his boyfriend for Christmas during college break, not his best friend Julia, the girl next door. At thirty-four and a second Lieutenant in the Marines, asking his men to keep killing in Bagdad didn't make sense to him anymore, though he loved his country and wanted to uphold the Marine slogan: "Semper Fidelis." "Always faithful." It was all coming up in the form of huge panic attacks when he returned to Davis, his home town. How could he face his father? What would he tell his three children? Whatever happened to his sex life with Joddie, his wife?

The first chakra is identity. This is the "Who Am I?" chakra. Our individuality is made up of the rich soup of our parent's DNA, our sexual orientation, cultural infusion and all the past lives, embedded with all its karma.

Our parents give us our first identity "We are the Jones family." Our parents give us the signals of what they expect from us. Here is where the seeds of expectations are planted. When my father would say, "You do it because I'm the father!" He was speaking from his first chakra. The only harm that can develop is when a parent feels they are only successful if the children do what they did or what they wanted. I have always suspected that if you have to prove yourself in a "family" situation, you have first chakra differences with your parents. If your first chakra values matched your parents, you wouldn't have to prove yourself.

When people develop a first chakra alliance with someone, it doesn't have to be sexual, but it is a very deep connection. In this type of friendship, whatever happens to them, you also feel is happening to you. It is the concept of one-for-all and all-for-one. It is a profound first chakra bonding. After working with many clients on their sexuality issues, I have come to the conclusion that most of our information concerning sexuality is carried in from the last lifetime and then mixed with the DNA of our parents. Occasionally, the DNA of this lifetime does not match the last lifetime experience and there is a sexual identity conflict in this lifetime.

Complicated, yes. The good news is, there is another round of life experience to resolve such issues, and then accept and go forth into this lifetime. The greatest leverage to living the good life is being present in every moment.

Traditions are events that help us survive in this chaotic world. As a young boy, Clyde wanted catfish for Thanksgiving, his mother was totally aghast. His father gave him a spanking. "How could he be so selfish, it's the one time of the year when everyone gets together to give thanks, not to act out." He remembered his grandmother mutter in the kitchen. "He's just a boy," was the only answer his grandmother could think of.

At least Clyde had not challenged the family religion. Changing your religious beliefs always threatens the family foundations. It is a huge test for a relationship, when partners are from different faiths, let alone experiencing spiritual development in different directions.

Placement is also a first chakra issue. Placement can be summed up in that old Southern question asked of every stranger, "Where ya' comin' frum?"

Every election tries first to establish placement. Where do you "stand" on basic issues. Most everybody wants their issues to be red, white and blue. You don't mix them. Clyde was a democrat and that made his father confused and disappointed. When he mixed those emotions together, it turned into pure anger. They were both jarheads, but all they could do with each other was grunt. The only thing they had in common as adults was the good taste of Jack Daniels.

Clyde wasn't proud to be a Marine anymore and it saddened him that he had to give up his father for his new-found concern for others. He had blindly placed his trust in an institution that didn't have the same core values he now held. It takes a strong person to be flexible. He could follow instructions, but he was aware of the cost of his actions. Clyde had developed some new spiritual skills he hadn't reckoned for in Bagdad. Simply, Clyde perceived that the wheel of Karma was round. If he was going to do that much killing of children, mothers, fathers; it was going to come home one day. He loved his country and followed in his father's footsteps by marching right into the Marine Corps. Now, he could not keep up the farce. He couldn't reconcile the killing of so many children over the price of gas or some sort of weapons of mass destruction that could never be found. He was panicked that someday he would have to pay for his actions. The wheel of Karma would turn and face him right where he lived. Here, every night in his dreams and the terror of waking each morning, he thought of the people he killed.

Clyde McKinley developed shingles, where his medal of honor used to hang on his dress uniform.

The first chakra loves drama, things and events that affect the first chakra are "larger than life events or issues." Clyde had pushed nearly all the buttons: career change, life threatening illness, loss of identity with family and county. No wonder he felt like he was going to die, since all of the above dealt with survival.

The question with this client was how to start moving the energy through his first chakra without the personality destroying itself from fear and illusion? I remembered one client who used sex with multiple partners to stimulate and move his energy from the first chakra upward. He was unaware of his subconscious flirting with the art of Tantric sex. One objective of Tantric sex is not to have an orgasm but send the energy to the next three charkas, thereby speeding up the vibration level of the second, third and fourth chakra. This process would cleanse the body and mind; allowing for new information to be embedded into the heart chakra. How the individual uses this new information is the material for great novels and cheap movies.

Having a child definitely changes how a woman views survival. When you accept the responsibility of another, you reflect on the actions that you have taken for the care of yourself and now another. You cannot give to another, what you have not given to yourself first. Having a child is an amazing reflection of the inner self, an overlay with another soul. One of the most intimate experiences a human can have is to become a mother or father.

Clyde wanted to live and shift into his natural evolving Self. That would take a true Marine. The courage to be honest with his wife about his sexual preference; a new career that would use his talents he could honor; accept himself and possible accept his father, the jarhead.

Clyde was ready for all the support he could get, traditional and non. I flipped the files and looked at different clients; all the folders contained data intake forms and drawings of energy patterns on their physical form. Flipping through the thick manila file dividers, Marilyn Frostbinder's file opened to her yellow colored data sheet and a drawing of her energetic system.

I sighed and reflected on the thought that all of my clients were hometown miracles to me.

Marilyn Frostbinder was no exception. She had been sent to me by one of the local doctors. It was a test. New healers in town are always tested. I was the new kid on the block. I had arrived in Davis a year ago from the East Coast and I had just opened my practice. It is my belief that traditional and non-traditional medicine compliment each other. My practice is run that way, one is no better than the other. During a person's healing process, best results can be obtained when a well-rounded approach is taken toward recovery. Doctor Richardson was testing my approach by referring one of his hopeless clients to me. Western medicine couldn't do any more for this one. The kind doctor was throwing out dead bait and wanted to see if I could fish with it.

Marilyn had lived in Marysville all her life. She had raised three sons and enjoyed the benefits of her retired husband's efforts as a teller at the Great Eastern Bank. She lacked nothing and wanted everything. She ate everything to fill herself, yet she was starving. She had a first chakra issue:

survival.

Her sessions always started with the topic of food. "You know, I only get vegetables from the Farmer's Market. Organic. Only organic. I wouldn't let my sons drink Coke either." She sighed, as her rounded shoulders curved even further to protect her delicate heart. "When they were growing up! My poor boys. They were ostracized, because I wanted to feed them only the best. natural foods. Whole grains, none of that junk food in their lunch boxes. They wanted to hide during lunch. Jeff and David. In fact, all my men thought I was so demanding. And yet, I just wanted the best for them." She made giggling sounds like a twelve-year-old.

Then the veins on her neck pulsated frantically. She sneezed and gasped for air. The deep lines on her forehead revealed years of physical pain that was now constant. The exacerbating pain traveled on a system not unlike the Manhattan subway: zipping past Canal Street to 34th Street.

As she laid on the massage table, her chest rose and fell sporadically. She wanted freedom from her torture and modern medicine had given her only pills to dull her senses. Marilyn couldn't make sense of anything now. In her last session, Marilyn quietly spoke of her dependency on Walter. Walter Frostbinder was her husband of twenty-seven years. She loved him, but in that time of loving and living, she had lost her edge to fight for what she wanted. It's not that she was too old, too frightened, too female. She was totally lost in the illusion of her dependency on Walter.

I was once told that Krishna, the Hindi God, the embodiment of love and destroyer of all pain, had to rescue his mother from Heaven. Marilyn was stuck in the illusion of that belief.

I tilted my head, to listen more deeply about her husband. Walter Frostbinder was more than retired from the bank, he was asleep. Marilyn's husband of twenty-seven years had provided for the family all too well and everyone applauded him, except her. The anger ate at her hands and hips. Her skin felt like dried up cabbage leaves. On the surface, she had forgotten part of herself. She was much more than a mother. Now all she remembered was "more." Marilyn's sausage fingers gripped the side of the table, as she turned to whisper her words that were wrapped in desperation and oozing with urgency, "Any kind of relief. Please."

A cold chi came over me and passed over my lips. I had seen this before. I had even known it once in my lifetime. Father Time had turned into Death and he was sitting on her chest. For some clients, it was a gray field that surrounded them. For others, it took the form of a holographic image of someone who first introduced them to the concept of death. It might have been an aunt or a neighbor down the street, who died when they were very young. Someone out there had to let them know it wasn't forever and sometimes I saw them.

That's why modern medicine couldn't help her. Neither could I in their eyes. Marilyn Frostbinder was dead bait in the water, but as long as she was alive, it was my responsibility to offer her the space to heal. You see she had the telltale sign of life: she was angry. That anger was killing her and it was her greatest hope.

I'm a believer and a fool. There is a great Mystery and on good days I follow the believer.

In this session, Marilyn's breathing became regular and the room transformed into pure silence. I got up from my listening chair, "Marilyn, I'm going to move down the left side of your body and start the energetic work. Balancing your body." I had circled her body once. Now again. My left-hand gliding twelve inches above her body, never touching her physical form. My interest was in the energetic field around her body and her first chakra. How strong was her survival chakra?

Her body twitched once and then again. She sighed. I went to the end of the table and held my left hand above her right foot and my right hand above her left foot. This process of balancing her chakras would pull and guide energy from her crown chakra all the way through her body and come out at the bottom of her feet. My body acted as a grounding rod to Mother Earth. If the session was going to take a bit of time, I would bring my chair to the end of the massage table and sit with my hands up in the air. The palms of my hands were parallel to her feet, but not touching her feet. While sitting in the chair, both the client and myself could go into a trance. Just before this would happen, the atmosphere in the room would become "thick," viscous by nature. It was as if the space between everything became very palpable. My sight expanded. I could see the energetic glow of the client's body. A golden light surrounded them. If they were sick or becoming cancerous, a gray film would appear around their body parts. During this time of extended sight, I would see these things. Some people are able to see the colors of the energetic field surrounding the human body, I could do this only while working on a client. The development of Kirlian photography has made it possible to confirm the presence of the energetic body around the living physical form.

Marilyn murmured and went into a deeper trance, as I sat in my chair. Suddenly, her true, authentic-self appeared to us both in the form of the most beautiful sound I had ever heard. At first, she created polyphonic overtones and within a few minutes began to sing a few lines from "Habanera."

Was she channeling André Rieu? Or was this a part of her higher self? Every muscle in my body was transfixed; I held my breath, hoping Marilyn would not stop singing.

Marilyn's chest swelled as she sang. Then her body convulsed. She shook her head, as if to remember who she had become. She came out of the trance. "My God! Where did that come from?" She covered her eyes in shame. "I've always, always wanted to sing. My mother loved opera music. Cleaning the living room, Pavarotti's voice would clean everything. My God, the sound just came out of my mouth!" With her left hand, she reached for the Kleenex laying on the massage table. She had been strong so long for her boys, she hadn't felt tears on her face for a quarter of a century. "I was going to go to music school, but I got pregnant with Jeffery. Everything changed. Walter and I got married after that. Everything, everything changed." She sniffled and took another Kleenex, "I love my boys."

Tears streamed out of her eyes, down her cheeks and made a pond in the indentation of her clavicle bone. These were the same tears which filled Carnegie Hall when Pavarotti sang. It was the only time and place a New Yorker could cry passionately after 9/11. Here were those same tears, in our town.

"What about now, Marilyn?" I said in my softest voice, only emphasizing the word "now." "Could you sing in the Church choir now? Have you ever taken singing lessons? What's happening at the Marysville Senior Center?" My mind was racing a mile a minute, trying to fix it, rather than letting life be perfect for one moment.

"No, it's gone. I could never." Her voice trailed off and she morphed back to her normal self. In pain, locked in place. She turned on her side and doubled up into the fetal position.

For one moment, she was free and able to do what she dreamed. The energy blocked in her first chakra, exploded and burst forth in her fifth, activating her creative potential in that energy vortex. This often happened to women during menopause. Three major events take place during menopause: firstly, hormonal changes; secondly, polarity shifts within the outer rim of the electromagnetic field of the female body, and thirdly, Kundalini energy that flows inside the body, which might have been used in the younger years for survival and creating children, now can surge upward and hit the mark of the fifth chakra. The fifth chakra, sometimes called the throat chakra, is about communication, creativity and judgment. This center rules self-expression and speaking one's truth. Imbalance in this center may be experienced as poor self-expression, habitual lying, learning disabilities, fear, and uncertainty. A balanced fifth chakra in a female after menopause can produce a Grandma Moses, the Peace Pilgrim, or help her become a Janet Rowley, discovering the activities of chromosomes that lead to discovery of cell malignancy. Now with four million women over 50 years old; we are going to witness a polarity shift that only women can do.

In the wink of an eye, a miracle happened, in the small-town call Davis.

Marilyn Frostbinder and I were both transported to Carnegie Hall. I heard the most amazing aria and Marilyn was her deep authentic-self.

Smiling at the remembrance of that event, I closed the first drawer with my right foot, then I opened the second file drawer with my left hand. The whole drawer was lined with orange colored wallpaper. It contained Cathy Randel's folder. She was coming next Tuesday. I picked the file up and remembered her in my mind's eye.

"Cathy Randal, Cathy Randal." She had second chakra issues. This was the chakra to discover how things existed side-by-side. It signified your placement in the world. To most people, they remembered the second chakra because it is related to the sex organs; our ability to "create and expand the self into family," This chakra aroused my curiosity on the topic of autism. If the first chakra concerned itself with internal placement, the second chakra has to do with the relationship to others. Internal love of the Self becomes "amore" and is expressed in the physical side of love. Here, in the second chakra, the passion of duality could rise, mix and expand in physical form.

Cathy had a classic stuck second chakra, with a wide-open seventh chakra. She had been a nun for twenty years and she looked it. If she could only find a hairdresser who saw past those years, she could be transformed. But heaven can only help those who help themselves. How could she conjure up a hairdresser who could save her if she never knew she needed to be saved? It's all a "Catch 22." Once you become aware of your need to be saved, then consciousness will come.

That Tuesday when Cathy walked into the healing room, I thought to myself, "Dear God, Cathy. When are you going to get a haircut?" I moaned as I leaned back against the black file cabinet and remembered her struggle with groups. The convent was a perfect place for her to hide out, while protecting herself. It was a classic need of these type of people; they either love or hate large crowds. A person with an open, sensitive second chakra; crowds of people will either feed or drain them. If a person is awakened to their second chakra needs, crowds could become a vibration symphony. For example, Madonna strutting her sexuality on stage, who expanded that energy though her singing voice, was amazing to watch. She never lost the sense of who she was. She was always fed by her audience.

This was not the case for Cathy. Like unprotected sex, a wide-open second chakra can affect a person's life for many years.

Cathy had spent her whole adult life protecting the second chakra and leaving the seventh chakra wide-open. First, she joined the convent, where she found others just like her who were looking to hide through God. The church also introduced her to the holy father of physics. There, in academia, at Notre Dame, God had appeared in His purist form, numbers. Ever expanding equations; the passion of duality in different "sets" of numbers; quantitative realities put into physical form; the sensual, visual aspect of a number. All of this sent her into a blissful state of reverie. She adored exploring the relationship of numbers, but couldn't stand to be in a relationship with humans. Especially men.

If the key phrase of the second chakra is "to honor one another," then Cathy was hiding from the other parts of herself. This chakra deals with expansion and the ability to discern what is safe and what isn't. In prehistoric times, this chakra was used to "tell" a human if the area was safe and what action to take. Fight or flight sits here. From this chakra comes the wisdom of "street sense." Every cab driver in New York City works their second chakra hard during a ten-hour shift. Every time a person steps into a cab, that driver has to assess what kind of a person just got in. If the cab driver isn't able to assess her passengers quickly, she could easily lose her life, if not all her earnings for that day. The second chakra is able to shield the body. If anger is sent toward us, it is normal to shield and run. This chakra wasn't supposed to judge emotions coming toward the physical form, just assess and take appropriate action.

When the second chakra is stuck, shattered or "slanted" toward its corresponding chakras, emotional information becomes skewed. There are problems with discernment between need, want and desire. Sex is a second chakra issue. Forty-eight women are raped every hour of the day, somewhere in the world. With this statistic, a large percentage of the world's female population will spend most of their lives healing their relationship to themselves and discovering how to "relate" to another human being.

While looking at Cathy's file, I thought of Max Rutgers. Max was complicated in his needs, but well supported by his parents and extended family. He had the grace of parents who knew the needs of a fourteen-year-old Asperger Syndrome child. Max hated crowds and was coming into puberty. Max and I were working on two major energetic issues: a wide-open second chakra and an over formulated kinesthetic processing field. In layman terms, Max was developing normally with his hormones and was extremely sensitive to the environment around him. He felt everything and that included girls. I remembered our sessions well.

"Goddamn Son of a Bitch!" Max folded his chubby hands over his extended belly. "Goddamn Son of a Bitch. I hate her. That's it." Max was having a second chakra fit. Like most young boys at that age, his ego was learning about the relationship between himself and the outer world, which was made harder still by his autism.

"I'm sorry, I didn't hear you." My comment startled him, he was yelling at the top of his lungs. "Could you repeat that?" I whispered, as I leaned in closer to his body, yet making sure I did not touch him. The close proximity would push his energetic field to the point of feeling prickly and would agitate him even more.

Max sucked in a huge wad of air, bent over backwards and sprayed it into my face, "Goddamn Son of A Bitch! That's her! Whadd ya' think I said?" It is best if a client can move the energy themselves; it allows for a quicker, safer movement of energy in their body. My smile broadened as I reflected on his mother's wise decision to offer Max two choices for the spring break: be on the soccer team and go to Reiki once a week or no more playing chess on the computer until school started again.

Max loved playing chess and hated girls. The game helped him expand intellectually without interacting with the opposite sex. Or anyone in fact. In Max's world, he was making all the right moves and winning. He was obsessed with chess and Chess Master, Robert Fischer. At the age of fourteen, Fischer had played in eight United States Championships, winning each one. By the age of sixteen, he was youngest Grandmaster and the youngest candidate for the World Championship. Max could relate to him like a brother.

With all this sitting while on the computer, Max was beginning to gain weight. Another problem, one side effect of the medication he took for anger, was also weight gain. He was putting on five pounds a month.

With hormones raging, anger overflowing and wanting to eat everything, Max was miserable. He had no idea how to address this new awareness of the opposite sex, let alone an awareness of himself. More and more his world was becoming a chess game. He was stuck inside a raging body and making all the wrong moves.

A Knight in the right place can hinder the development of the Bishop; where was Bobby Fischer now when Max needed him?

With the cooperation of his parents and regular visits to my office, Max was going to learn three things: firstly, the fine art of physical awareness through internal and external boundaries; secondly, the introduction of balancing his energy through Reiki and flower essences. "Well!" he yelled as his piggy short feet dangled from the massage table, as he stared at the floor. His mind was gathering words that he could fling at me like hot pokers.

"Well is a deep subject." Now I turned my head, "I predict you're going to be a star soccer player this spring. Mister." I watched to see if he would take the bait.

"No way. Really, I could beat that fucker, Melissa with the red-flaming-ass-hair? You know, there isn't a girl who has won the World Chess Championship." He smirked as he turned his head to look at the ceiling.

I diverted his perseverating about chess by giving him a direct instruction in present time, "Lie back down on the Reiki table and let me transfer some energy." I placed my right hand near his forehead while my left hand hovered over his stomach. There was no need to touch the body. For the longest while, Max's breathing was erratic, then it quieted down into an even pace. Finally, his body was synchronized with the universal energy directed by my hands.

Thirty minutes later, "There we go. We are finished." His body was balanced. It seemed like a nanosecond, but time was wrapped around a deep presence of the now. The whole experience felt weird to Max. "Weird and good," he would say. The Reiki treatment would allow him to experience a deep sense of physical balance in the present moment.

"Now, I want you to close your eyes and look at the soccer field, you just played on. See the two teams? Remember how we talked about visualization techniques? Be there. Are you in your uniform? Can you smell the grass? It is a wonderfully sunny day. The grass had just been cut. Can you smell it? Right!" He took a deep breath and as he exhaled, a big smile crossed his face. "Let your feet touch the ground. Feel your shoes slide across the grass. There are trees that line the left side of the field. Can you feel their coolness and the hardness of the metal goal posts?" I waited for a moment as I watched the fluttering of his eyes, behind his eyelids. "Now lift that soccer field and put in the sky. Take a deep breath. Take your favorite chess board. The one your father lets you keep in your bedroom. This isn't going to be hard. I want you to put the chess board on top of the soccer field. Can you do that?" His eyes fluttered frantically. "It's all right."

"Visualize the whole experience as a chess game. Now the other soccer players are going to become the chess pieces."

His ability to keenly focus on a certain topic, which was an autistic strain for some, coupled with his highly kinesthetic awareness, and his natural developing hormones could work together to create another hometown miracle. Max Rutgers could become a soccer star in Davis, California.

After working with Max for twenty more minutes, I saw him shiver and shake his head. His train of thought was broken. "My father is coming." Max could "feel" the presence of his father or anyone, four blocks away. Soccer would help him learn how to manage his acute "feeling" of others. He shook his body and jumped off the massage table. "He's almost here. I can feel him." Like clockwork, his father knocked on the pane glass window of the office door. With an impish smile, his father called out in a sheepish voice, "I'm here." There was a forced lightness in his voice. He so wanted to be accepted by his only son. Max's father was a farmer, who grew tomatoes, acres and acres of tomatoes. Their family had grown rich by using the right chemicals and fertilizers to grow their crops. But his father worried about all the "right chemicals" he used on his land. The questions kept him awake at night. Did these chemicals affect Max some how? What caused Autism and why my son?

"I know, Dad. I know." Max slumped, shoulders bowing forward and eyes looking upward at the corner of the room. Max never looked directly at his Dad. Looking directly at his father made him sad and visually confused.

Autism is a complex neurodevelopmental phenomenon that has several common characteristics, social interaction difficulties, communication challenges and tendency to engage in repetitive behavior. Each autistic individual differs to the extent in which they have these symptoms. Sometimes there is an increased intellect or deficit, but the universal core disability in autism, appears to focus on social functioning, awareness of self and dysfunctional firing of mirror neurons.

I once had a discussion with Nitya Chaitanyanand, a visionary in the area of human development. Her interpretation of the rise of autism would change my whole approach to working with autistic people.

"You see, dear," Nitya would say, as her right eyebrow would arch like the golden arches that appeared all over America. "Now. listen. The human species is in the process of making a quantum genetic leap. NOW, it's happening, Now! Some scientist and spiritualist are very aware of that process. Leo over at the Center for the Mind Institute, used to remind me that we've learned more about the brain in the last decade than the entire history of the world. He would compare his team of researchers to the Wright brothers." Her right hand made a circle in the air to emphasize the world and its shape. "Those scientists. Researchers. What are they anyway! So quick to judge what's happening in the brain and human body. They need to label everything. There is panic in the air for all the wrong reasons. This idea of 'disorder,' Good Heavens. Dis- order, how dis-tasteful! When a baby is learning to walk, after it stumbles and falls for the forty-first time, you don't say, 'Well, that one has a disorder' No. No. You pick the little one up, pat them on their behind and with a smile, say, 'Let's try that again.' Soon they are walking, and running, and you're chasing around trying to catch them."

For a moment, she stopped and sighed, "But there are two foibles this time around in the genetic up swing." Nitya was staring out into space, as if the room could hold the Milky Way and she was trying to see some far-off galaxy. "It's so sad. The first problem is environmental pollution, with the farming here. And the pollution in Delhi! There is no air in Delhi…. It's too hazy, gritty, all the way to Hardwar." She sighed, missing her home, and then went back to her discourse, "And then there's the genetic factors of parents who are having babies. I was visiting friends in the Yurok Tribe up north. There are no elders. Everyone is dying off early because of diabetes. Gray Dove was the last Elder. She left her body last year. Gone at fifty-five. Dear God, I was just getting started in life at fifty-five. The babies coming into pre-school are pre-diabetic! DAMN! These two factors alone have polluted the genetic soup at the very least. Let's say one out of every 70 boys born in the last hour are autistic," she said, and sighed. I hadn't heard her use vulgarity for a long time. She was schooled in England. Her English, Hindi and four other languages were impeccable. There was no room for harsh words in her vocabulary. "There are more and more babies being born with abnormalities. One in thirty-eight babies born in northern California are "pre" something before they start kindergarten. What are we to do? Well!" And she made the same circle with her right arm outstretched, index finger pointing down as if to stir the cosmic pot counter clockwise. "Please, give us some sort of intervention on the birthing process to get us back into clockwise ascension…" Now both of her eyebrows were arched, as her arm furiously swung in a clockwise circle. This time her index finger was pointing upward. "Or will we wake up to a wave of human awareness concerning our health? Maybe islands of recovery for mothers will be created. Places people can go to retreat and heal their bodies. You know what I mean." She would always use that phrase, "You know what I mean!" after trying to describe some global insight that was multi-layered and would take hours to verbally unravel.

My memory of Nitya was jarred by Max kicking the black file cabinet for attention. I looked at the top of his head, not to confront him. "Next week, Max. Same time. Mr. Same Time." Max turned and with no goodbye, walked out of my office, father in tow. His father tried to catch the door as Max slammed it.

I chuckled and sighed deeply. After all that mental work, now Max was going to have fun. Max the soccer star. With the use of some Australian Bush Flower remedies, his sensitive body would be supported, as energy would be directed upward to his third chakra. This chakra is located above the navel or slightly below the solar plexus. The gift of this chakra is sensing your personal power, being confident, responsible, and reliable. The third chakra is the center of your self-esteem, willpower, self-discipline, as well as warmth in your personality. That is why it has been called the Manipura, by the Hindu people: the "City of Jewels": Mani –gem and Puri meaning city.

This is a chakra that very few people talk about in practical terms or with the understanding of "Karma". Walter Makichen knew how to teach about the chakra system in very practical terms. Going to his seminars, I learned a great deal about the practical side of the Chakra system.

Walter was an amazing teacher, clairvoyant, and spiritual philosopher. He was the founder of a meditation center in Sacramento. His wife described him as a "practical, pragmatic guy from Philly, who just happened to embrace a spiritual life." I had the pleasure of hearing him speak and lead meditations. He did an in-depth seminar on chakras in 1997. I spoke with him often about the chakra system and Reiki.

For Walter, the third chakra is the "enforcer." Energy from the second chakra flows up into the third and energy from the sixth chakra flows down into the third. From our past lives and acquired Karma, we learn and determine what is acceptable or not for survival. Nitya would describe Karma as "the sum of a person's actions in this and previous states of existence that influence a person's fate in future existences."

The third chakra was a library of this Karmic information. Karma is explicit; from our past we learn, "This is how we do it. These are the rules." This chakra takes that information and determines what rules should be followed in this present lifetime for survival. The third chakra manifests those rules by our physical action and by our emotional expression. The chakra gives the body energy to follow through on those rules. It gives permission to say and act in the world. Or not act.

There are many signs of the third chakra being weak and malfunctioning. The major sign is that a person sees themselves as powerless, submissive, passive. People with weak third chakras will often use shame as a way of sabotaging themselves. What others will think of them is more important than what they think of themselves. Third chakra "bleeders" are very goal oriented. If they are not going after something bigger, better, the best, they feel hollow, empty. They are driven, frantically trying to cover up the third chakra hole inside. They are bleeders because they drain their adrenal glands, create ulcers and the pancreas pushes the system into diabetes or hypoglycemia.

If a person has spent ten lifetimes learning how to please others, as well as the ones you love to survive, then it is very hard to become an independent person in this lifetime. In this lifetime, your third chakra is hardwired to please and think of others first. That is how you survived in the past. Some would say, "No problem, right?" Wrong.

Philosophers have described this earth as a school. We come to learn and evolve. What would happen if in this lifetime you met a teacher, started to meditate, went into therapy, had a life- altering experience that changed your perception of the "shoulds" in your life.

What if?

What if change happened as it always does, and you didn't want to please everyone so much. What if you wanted to come first?

Joan Godshaw was a classic blocked third chakra kinda gal. At forty-three, she looked like Peggy Lee at her last performance in Las Vegas, ready to sing "Is That All There Is?" When Joan smiled, the sun tried to shine extra bright. Little rays of "Can I help you?" seemed to follow her everywhere, but never touched her.

Her stomach hurt. There were one hundred pounds of Karmic sludge from the waste water treatment plant of her life packed into her third chakra. She could hardly move and the backup didn't stop at the duodenum, jejunum or ileum. It took three sessions to mention her God-awful hemorrhoids.

Literally, Joan couldn't stomach it any more. That's why she came to me. Nothing could help her stomach. Joan wanted to eat the world and she knew that she was pre-diabetic. She had gone to doctors and attempted every diet possible. The famous Grapefruit Diet. The Akins Diet. The Ultra Low-Fat Diet. The Paleo Diet. Nothing worked.

After several sessions of trust building through Reiki sessions; Joan had revealed she wanted to change, but nothing inside her would listen or move. The closer she got toward transformation, the more she would eat. If your mouth is full, it's hard to talk about it.

"And what was that change? What was it?" I asked.

"I'm going to die. Lose all my friends. And I'm so tired." Joan brought her right hand up to her mouth. It looked like she was trying to put an imaginary chocolate fudge cupcake with white frosting into her mouth. She licked her lips and felt her lips to see if there were any phantasmic chocolate crumbs to brush away with her little ring finger. "I'm so tired. I've done enough for all of them and I'm scared to ask for anything. I want a crumb. Just a little something for me."

From my end of the table, she looked like a beached Beluga Whale. This was going to take more than energetic work. I was thankful she had a good therapist and was ready to take some personal action with the help of her husband. She was in one of those now or never places. She couldn't go back to her old habits and yet was hysterical about taking personal action toward something new.

I decided that one of my tools would be the Australian Bush Flower Essences. I had great success with these remedies. Joan loved traveling to Australia. Sidney was her favorite city, next to Manhattan. With the personal work she was doing with her therapist and an affinity for Australia, these essences would act as a catalyst to move her blocked third chakra.

The creator of the Australian Bush Essences is Ian White. He is a fifth-generation herbalist and his great-grandmother was an herbalist in the Australian Gold Rush in 1850. He has carried on the family tradition and health practitioners all over the world use the flower essences in their practices.

In his book, Australian Bush Flower Essences, he describes how the essences have their effect on the physical body; "When an essence is ingested, it is initially assimilated into the bloodstream. Then, it settles midway between the circulatory and nervous system. There, an electro-magnetic current is created by the polarity of the two systems. The essence then moves directly to the meridians. From the meridians, the life force of the flower essence is amplified out to the chakras."

For Joan, there would be a need for a "bouquet" of flower essences. First, the flower essence made from the shrub Styphelia Triflora, would work well. This flower is also called the Five Corners. It is a tall shrub that gets its name from its fruit which has five corners This essence allows the life force to flow through major centers of the body. My clients told me that this essence helped them with their self-esteem and lack of confidence.

Added to the Five Corners, would be The Tall Yellow Top essence. Ian had described this essence for alienation. When there is no feeling of connection to self, family or community, Ian would prescribe Tall Yellow Top. The biological name is Senecio Magnificus. This essence would promote a sense of belonging, acceptance of one's self and the ability to reach out, ask for what was needed.

The last essence in her bouquet would be Callistemon Linearis. I like the common name: Bottlebrush. There are twenty species of this flowering bush and they mostly grow in New South Wales, Australia. The shrub prefers damp soil and can grow to be ten feet tall. The flowers are packed together in a cylindrical shape, literally looking like a red colored bottlebrush. It reminded me of the brush with a long thin handle that my mother would use to clean glass milk containers.

This essence would help Joan clean out the past and move forward with her life. She would also need support for her adrenal that had been pushed to the limit. For that, I consulted with Laura Done, an innovative medical Naturopath from Oregon. She suggested that Joan do an Ion Cleanse once a month, while she was losing weight. This cleansing process would clean her body, while the flower essences shifted her psyche.

In my office, I tried to explain to Joan how the Ion Cleanse worked, "The ion foot detox process has been used by many health practitioners to help detox the body and make the body's pH level more alkaline. The importance of the body being alkaline is crucial to a person's health. Diseases thrive in an acidic environment. The less acidic the body is, the less prone a person is to contracting a disease. The body functions best when the ions are balanced at 80% negative and 20% positive. Most of the time, the body gets its pH balance through our food intake and what we drink.

The Ion Cleanse operates through a process called electrolysis. This is done by generating the proper amount of current in the water causing the water molecules to divide producing negative ions. Once the negative ions are present in the water, the body absorbs these ions through osmosis. This enhances the body's ability to cleanse itself internally and naturally at an increased rate. The ions neutralize microscopic particles that can easily pass through the skin and tissues of the body.

"I hate doing these detoxes. And I don't totally understand what you just said. It freaks me out!" said Joan, whining before she placed her feet in the basin full of water and the Ion Cleanse processor. "Last time it was dark green, with flecks of black on the bottom of the basin. What was that white foam floating on the top toward the end?" She looked down at her feet, as if they might not be hers.

"The green color is detoxification of the gallbladder. The black flecks are heavy metals. Let's see, yes. The foam means your lymphatic system is releasing. You're doing a whole lot of work there." I smiled in amazement of what the body could store and what we could physically release.

"But I did feel better after the last session. I slept deeply that night.," Joan sighed and closed her eyes to remember that night of bliss.

Then I closed my eyes for a moment, too. Would she be another home-town miracle? Could she change patterns that had lasted over several lifetimes or shift deep-rooted habits in this lifetime? The question is: could she break away from those patterns to start new grooves within her thought patterns? This would take diligent, consistent work on her part. Human beings like repetition. Sameness is comforting. Change is hard. Effort and time would tell.

That thought made me pull open the fourth drawer on the filing cabinet that night. After supper and once the office was clean, I thought about tomorrows client: Christopher. What are we going to do with you, Christopher? His was a classic tale of a heart broken in two. Or was his heart really broken?

Christopher Hedgewyck was British. He had met the love of his life at Yale University, while doing his doctorate work on quantum information processing. He had always been fascinated by Schrodinger's theory of the cat. Christopher was fully engaged in creating harmonic oscillating states in his laboratory. Could Schrodinger's cat live in two different boxes at the same time? It seemed Christopher's whole intellectual life was taken up with this thought. Then one day while taking a break from the lab and people watching, he saw Emilie. One look and he knew she was the one. That "one" meant: dating, engagement, proposal, marriage and having children, all in one breath.

It almost happened that quickly. Her family adored him. Emilie was so flattered to be the total focus of this handsome, brilliant young man on scholarship from Great Brittan. Were they soul mates, she wondered.

The first time he came to my office, he marched right to the massage table and plopped down. He swung his legs back and forth. Christopher's brown, highly polished Oxford shoes made a squeaking sound, as he swung his legs and let his shoes scuff the floor. He closed his eyes and started to recite his marriage vows, "Today we have come together to witness the joining of these two lives. For them," his throat tightened, but he still went on," For them, out of the routine of ordinary life, the extraordinary has happened. Romance is one thing, but true love is something far more and it is their desire to love each other for the rest of this lifetime. I will trust you and honor you. I will laugh with you and cry with you. Through the best and the worst. Whatever may come I will always be there. As I have given you my hand to hold." And then Christopher laid down in fetal position and started to cry. No, not cry, he began to sob violently. Men rarely cried in my office; they would sob when their time came and his was now. His whole body shook savagely.

"She broke my heart." He wailed, clutching his chest with both hands.

If the first three chakras give us structure, the fourth has none. You might say, "It just is." The heart chakra accepts everything that could happen. The heart says you can do anything; you will never be defeated; anything is possible. The heart cannot judge. Life just is.

My good friend and Hindi teacher, Rucki, would give instruction over the phone to me. "Yes, the heart. You must understand, Anahata is associated with the ability to make decisions outside the realm of Karma."

She would roll the R in realm and accentuate the K in Karma. "In Mani-pura, we are bound by the laws of Karma and fate. Am I right?" That was never a question, it was a rhetorical moment for students to answer yes and refocus on what Reiki was emphasizing. "In Anahata, you can make decisions based on one's higher self. Not emotional stuff and desires. Do you understand?" That was a question.

I would sigh and say, "Yes." All the while asking myself, how could I understand something so difficult to achieve as to have an open heart? But here I was trying to help someone with a somewhat broken ego and an unknown, gracious heart. Christopher loved people. He didn't care who they were, Their shape, size, color, education. He was blind to judgment. Christopher liked people for who they were. People were much like Schro-dinger's cat; he would muse, "Such a mystery."

Christopher loved his Emilie. Her cooking was as grand and myste-rious as physics. There was hardly a dinner that Emilie cooked just for two. Christopher would also bring home someone from the lab. They were on a budget and she would work magic. Corn and cheddar soufflés with kale. A side dish of mushroom salad; asparagus tempura tacos; fresh corn on the cob, smothered in butter, with smoked paprika and lime zest. She was just as inventive as he was. Who would have thought of making the "garden patch special" of fennel, basil and gin? Everyone loved her "red alert" served at cocktail hour, made of beet juice, sliced fresh horseradish and cheap vodka- a drink that would clear any physicist's head.

"What happened?" He would wail, shifting his body from left to right.

"Get off the massage table, before you fall off. Who has insurance?!" He was exacerbating the situation with all his drama. "Lie down on the mat. God help us all." He was throwing around energy everywhere, with total disregard for other human beings. I thought the British didn't have emotions and yet here he was -hysterical, and related to the First Earl of Pembroke.

He rocked from side-to-side-to-side on the mat. "What happened?!" he moaned in his stilted Wilton accent. He was born in Wilton, England. Wilton is five miles west of Salisbury and known for the Wilton House. His great relative, the Earl of Pembroke, built the Wilton House. It was all Tudor, on the grounds of a defunct Benedictine Abbey. It was ruined by fire in 1647 and now Christopher was burning up, too.

What happened? "Life happened," is what I wanted to say, but didn't. He couldn't hear me now. Christopher was still burning with desire. He so wanted the reality that he had made up of Emilie to be alive and well.

The third chakra is about morality; expectations of good and bad, in and outside of us. But the heart could never answer "why" of anything because it can accept everything. The heart says, "Anything goes. Anything could happen." Maybe that is why Christopher loved Schrodinger's quantum theory. The cat could be dead or alive. He wouldn't know until he opened the box and looked in. Until you observe and take action, there's a paradox. Christopher observed Emilie with an open heart and told his mind, "Anything can happen. She's the one!" One glance and he was in love. She was the one who would fulfill his heart's desires.

He had taken the chance and opened the box of love. He had lived the Schrodinger experiment and here he was.

Emilie jumped out of the box, and then, in time, ran away. Christopher so wanted the idea of Emilie. She was the same. She wanted the tall, good looking physicist from Wilton, England. She did not want the man named Christopher Hedgewyck, who was related to the Earl of Pembroke. When realities shift or worse, dissolve, the ego can become uncomfortable, even frantic. Christopher's problem was not so much his heart as his mind. Because Emilie had violated the marriage contract, Christopher thought she had broken his heart, but it was his ego that was broken. There was a marriage contract and this was what they were to follow. It was a solid, workable foundation. That is what his ego and personality told him.

"By God, we are going to figure this out." I was fearful that the next statement coming out of his mouth would be, "God save the Queen!"

But Christopher's heart travels from moment to moment, in the wonderment of possibilities, never judging, always hopeful, not a rational chakra.

With this in mind; a bouquet of flower essences and energy work would be the beginning of his healing. I had chosen the Australian Bush Flower Remedies, a bouquet called "Relationship Essence." The flowers that make up this bouquet are: Bluebell, Bush Gardenia, Dagger Hakea, Mint Bush, Red Suva Frangpani, Boab and Flannel Flower.

The flower Bluebell grows in Kata Tjuta, which was formally The Olgas. The Olgas is now a National Park in Australia that protects a group of large ancient rock formations. The land and its rock formations are sacred to the Anangu people, who have inhabited the area for more than 22,000 years. The sandstone dome formation of the Kata Tjuta are said to be 500 million years old. Here in this ancient land, the Bluebells grow. I have followed Ian Whites suggestions for using the Bluebell Essence and gotten good results. This Essence helps to open the heart.

The Bush Gardenia can help a dying relationship to be revived. The Red Suva Frangipani grows on the coast near Darwin, Australia. Ian White has described the smell of this flower as being musky. He has used this flower essence when a client has had a loss of a deep relationship. This flower essence would help Christopher with his emotional upheaval.

The Dagger Hakaea is a flower which comes from a straggly bush that is found in the heathland areas of Australia. In his books, Ian often talked about using this essence when there was bitterness and deep resentment toward someone you loved. This essence can be used by itself when doing the process called "forgives and releases." Sally Perry taught this ceremony of "forgiveness and releases" to all her students. She and I both felt there could be no true healing without this process of forgiving and releasing anger, resentment, all that was held in the heart. I had often used this technique of forgiveness with my clients. It gave structure to the concept of letting go. For now, this Essence was good for Christopher in the relationship bouquet.

The Mint Bush would be needed during this time of confusion. Christopher had talked about a feeling that everything was all too hard. He couldn't deal with work and all the emotions that kept welling up, from nowhere. He was wearing a wet blanket that he couldn't take off, except when he laid on the massage table and allowed me to do energetic work with him.

"It's all so heavy. It's all too much to deal with and figure out," he would moan.

The Boab Tree is found in only one place in Australia and Ian has described this flower essence as one of the most powerful of all of all the essences he had discovered. Ian felt that this essence could clear negative emotional and mental patterns that were in a person's psyche for several life times. This flower essence was going to be one of the most potent in the bouquet.

The last flower essence in the relationship bouquet was the Flannel Flower. Trust had been broken and this would help him with this issue.

The energy work we would do could balance his chakras and bring about a "state" of wellbeing; giving him space to look at the relationship. Later on perhaps Christopher would approach the realm of forgiveness and look at expectations he had placed on the marriage. It was amazing how the Flower Essences complimented the energetic work.

Thinking about relationships and Christopher made me start to hum lines that Frank Sinatra used to sing, about how he fell in love with love itself and had eyes that couldn't see. I cleared my throat and tried to remember more of the lyrics.

CHAPTER TWELVE

"The Flower of Life"

All chakras take in energy and give it out. This function of a chakra is easiest to see in the fifth chakra. Its purpose is to translate and communicate. We take in information by listening and give it out by speaking. The fifth chakra is located in the throat area and includes the ears and eyes. It takes vibration energy forms and translates them into something we know. For example, if a person is hungry, this chakra will take this information and translate it into the thought form that they would hear inside, "I'm hungry. I need to eat." For some autistic individuals, like Temple Grandin, that information would be translated into pictures: the kitchen, steak, glass of milk. She would then know she was hungry and she'd better get something to eat.

My introduction to working with the fifth chakra was with my friend Richard. Every time Richard tried to speak the truth about what was in front of him, he got a frog in his throat. A very large frog in his throat. In fact, he collected frogs. Stuffed frogs, stone frogs, frogs on rubber stamps, frogs cut out of wood, frogs that were painted forest green with yellow polka dots. His kitchen was filled with them. A person couldn't put down a plate at the kitchen table for fear of crushing one. "Richard, you must come to my office for Reiki. I can't do it in your house." I feared being eaten alive by frogs.

Richard sold air time at the local radio station. I mused to myself that he was doing his own fifth chakra karmic work. Since he could not speak for himself, he practiced selling airtime to others.

The fifth chakra holds the past history of "how" a person will communicate to others. In this data base are the universal laws of the should and should not be said, of what is appropriate to be said, when and where. There are many overlays of rules from our past in this chakra.

Richard's greatest desire was to communicate with God. He told me that every morning when he awoke, the first thought that came out of his mouth was, "God, what do you want me to do today?" Every time he asked in prayer, the answer he wanted didn't come back exactly as he heard it. So he kept asking.

How you form a question will determine a great deal of what kind of answer you will get. Along with asking, is the art of listening. Richard had been locked in the fury of deeply asking and there was little room to listen for answers. Being a stubborn man with little imagination, life had to fit exactly as his ego wanted it to or nothing at all. All Richard could see were frogs. There wasn't another animal totem in his kingdom who could help. That is what he thought and so it was.

If only Rickard would listen with an open mind about Dr. William Condon's research in communications. It would have opened doors for him. One afternoon on the patio in front of my office, I talked with Richard about some ideas of Condon's research. "In a nut shell, Richard, Dr. Condon proved that people were keenly connected to each other through the spoken word. Just by asking a question, Dr. Condon felt we were connected to the answer."

Richard couldn't grasp the idea that Dr. Condon was working on, that when people spoke to each other they were in complete physical accordance with each other. They were dancing together mentally and physically. Richard didn't trust people, let alone his inner voice. That is why he only spoke to God. But God wasn't answering his questions correctly and every time he wanted to speak, there was that dry, froggy cough.

Richard loved to dance. Every Thursday night he would ride his light weight Schwinn to the university bar named the Graduate and order one

Samuel Smith's organic Sparkling Pear Cider. On the dot of seven o'clock line dancing would start. Richard would step in line and be in bliss.

"Richard, do you remember Sam Gersome. He went to Boston University, the same place Dr. Condon did his research. This guy Condon had analyzed people communicating with each other on video. Get this! When he slowed the video down, he noticed that body movements of both the listener and the speaker were in precise synchronicity with each other when they were in "peak" communication. Body movement of both persons changed as vowels were spoken. When people talk to one another, they are literally dancing with each other. Isn't that amazing?" Richard was silent.

For a moment, I reflected on the fact that Richard had a brother who was autistic. With some autistic individuals, there is a lag time between the response of the autistic person and the person they are interacting with. I had read an article about "mirror neurons" and how they worked in an autistic person. These neurons fire almost simultaneously within each person when they are communicating with each other. The person who acts and the person who receives the information are in a dance. It all starts in our brain, where neurons fire. These neurons "mirror" behavior of the other person. In autism, these neurons are damaged or do not exist. They are forever out of step with the world, because of their inability to synchronize with the world around them. Richard's case was not that different; but on a spiritual level, Richard's personality was not synchronized with his "Higher Self," a concept that Dr. Smith and Bill Wilson developed when creating Alcoholics Anonymous.

In everyday terms, Richard was not honest with himself and that had created a firewall of fear around him. We cannot completely heal ourselves, if we are not honest within. Many healers and motivational speakers focus on the "forgiveness" aspect of healing and never touch on the realm of honesty and truthfulness. If forgiveness is an energetic release, then being honest with one's self is the mechanism that retrieves energy back to the self for correct use.

Reiki sessions allowed Richard to energetically walk through his firewall of fear and honesty to face himself. Richard had made some economically bad choices that were fear-based. Those choices had led to what he wanted but had cost his relationship with his Higher Self or some would even say- his soul. Caroline Myss eloquently discusses the concept of surrendering the personal will to a higher source in her book, Anatomy of the Spirit.

Fear was the frog in Richard's throat. He had been trying to clear it for thirty-eight years. This year, once a week, Richard came to my office where he felt safe and began to speak his truth. Our sessions always started with a meditation, which lead into Reiki and ended with him speaking his truth in that moment. The meditation allowed Richard to quiet his mind. The Reiki gave him energy to break through his doubts and witness his divine connection with a source larger than himself. Speaking his thoughts out loud during the session allowed him to communicate and practice the physical act of working the fifth chakra.

Within a month, I added the Australian Flower Essence Red Lily. Ian White had described it as "the same flower that was the Sacred Lotus in the Buddhist tradition. It is for spirituality and connection to God in a grounded and centered way."

After three months of working together, Richard started to meditate every day, to quiet his mind from his internal chatter. He loved it and joined a local meditation class.

If Richard was connecting his fifth Chakra energy to his Higher Self, I reflected on a client whose mother was from Lithuania. This client was trying to become quiet enough to listen. We often think that people who are good talkers, are good listeners. Not necessarily.

Ruta was a constant talker. There was so much to be said. She had a doctorate in the minutiae of life. She used it to cover up the stories her mother tried to tell her about Paneriai.

Ruta's mother had emigrated to American right after the Second World War. With her mother came grandmother, three sisters and four aunts, who had lost their husbands and sons to the invasion of their homeland. A murder of Lithuanian women, all in silent black - crowing in bitterness, but never to be heard. Ruta's grandfather had died in a deportation camp in Germany. Her father was never spoken of, he was gone. "Where did his soul fly to?" Ruta asked.

"They came in the night," was all her mother kept repeating, as her sky-blue eyes would cloud over from her internal war. "They came in the night," she would say, rocking back and forth, holding baby Ruta. "They came in the night," whispered her mother, as she braided her hair when Ruta was fourteen.

Christmas was a nightmare for Ruta. The singing of Silent Night always reminded Ruta of her mother's words about father. To get through the holiday, she would constantly hum to herself; she heard nothing but the buzz and whooping sound of her internal bee. When she was young, she made a pet of her internal bee; coming and going at her command. When she turned fifteen and started to bleed; the bee went crazy. Without moving her mouth or taking a deep breath into her lungs, a buzzing sound would come inside her head. The bee was lost and constantly bumping up against the inside of Ruta's brain. "How is it going to get out, away from the night?" Ruta would say to herself.

As the noise inside grew, there became a need for her external world to also have a buzz. In Ruta's apartment, the TV was always on. She loved watching "Cheers." Every Saturday night, the radio would blare out "Open House Party," and she could not miss "The Future Hits." There wasn't any space for a silent night.

Ruta grew exhausted, blocking any form of silence. She had learned that silence has layers, just like a mille-feuille pastry. You have to eat mille-feuille, a little bite at a time. Layer-upon-layer: three layers of pâte feuilletée, then two layers of pastry crème, with the top layer dusted with sugar or cocoa. These complex favors cannot be savored all at once. It was the same with our sessions.

We started with me playing the crystal bowls while she lay on the massage table. It was like the top layer of the mille-feuille; with a dusting of cocoa. The sound of the crystal bowl is made by the vibration of galvanized silica sand which is pure quartz in nature. The bowls are made by dropping silica sand into a centrifugal spinning mold and in the center of the mold an electrical arc torch is ignited to several thousand degrees centigrade. The silica sand melts and becomes a crystal bowl.

The sound from the bowl is made by rubbing a wooden stick covered with suede, around the edge of the bowl. The friction causes a harmonic tone. The faster I rub the stick around the edge of the bowl, the more it would begin to sing. Silica is part of our bone structure and when we listen to a crystal bowl, the vibration of the bowl aligns with the silica in the bones of our body. The effect of this action may be: relaxation, going into trance, acute activation of the senses, even falling into a deep sleep. It all depends on the individual, frequency of the bowl, the practitioner and one hundred and one other elements that might unfold during the playing of the crystal bowls to reveal the unforeseen.

For Ruta the sound of the bowl relaxed her body instantly. I usually played for twenty minutes. During the first three sessions, she fell into a deep sleep and always awoke, rubbing her smiling eyes that had become clear blue. In the fourth session, she was talking in chunks. I would listen to the gaps of silence between her words and phrases. Listening and trying to discern inflections and different lengths of silence between words is a fine art form. This information always gives me clues about a person's subconscious expression of emotions.

The process of listening to silence was awakened in me by experiencing the performance of the renowned piano virtuoso, David Tudor, playing John Cage's creative piece 4' 33". David Tudor walked onto the stage at Carnegie Hall, sat down at the Steinway piano and took a big breath. Then he opened the keyboard lid, sat in silence for several minutes and then closed the keyboard lid. He did this three times; then when the silence enveloped the whole auditorium, he stood up and left the stage.

The performance was riveting. It changed the experience of silence for everyone in the audience, including me.

Now it was my turn to listen to Ruta's riveting performance of silence. When Ruta revealed layers of her fearful past, her own devilish mille-feuille, I listened for the markers of her healing process, the silence that grew in the healing room.

Ruta's sensory gating was flawed, like many of the autistic adults I saw. Sensory gating describes neurological processes of filtering out redundant or unnecessary stimuli in the brain from all possible environmental stimuli. I discovered there was a fracture in Ruta's ability to filter interior and exterior information. By now the world had turned past the age of information, into an age of discernment, Ruta struggled with this process. The Webster Dictionary describes the word discern as the "ability to value something at a glimpse; to decide, to first examine everything carefully."

Slowly, silence was becoming her filter of discernment.

Silence wrapped her body in awareness, giving Ruta the ability to discern her interior life from the external world. In the eighth session, there was a need to administer something for the physical form. During this session, I would play the bowls, administer Reiki and listen. Now the shift. Play the bowls, Reiki, listen, and add a few drops from a bouquet of flower essences created by Ian White, the Australian naturopath. The bouquet was made up of Fringed Violet, Sun Shine Wattle and Kapok Bush.

Bowls, Reiki, drinking of the flower essences in a glass of water, listen and wait. That was the formula.

Every practitioner needs a large dose of "Wait and listen" in their healing tool bag. Patience is a cultivated healing form that never comes easily and is usually dressed in superior beliefs. I needed more "wait," less "show and tell."

The Australian Flower Essence Fringed Violet would help Ruta with her damaged aura. In his book, Australian Bush Flower Essences, Ian White describes the Fringed Violet, as one of twenty different Thysanotus species found in every state of Australia except one. It is a tall, slender plant that can grow up to fifteen feet high. It has grass like leaves and beautiful purple flowers.

Ruta's aura had been stretched very thin, because of the genetic trauma her mother and grandmother had experienced. All three women had thin, frail auras. Life in Lithuania was very traumatic. Too many wars, with too little taste of independence. How could Ruta and her heritage feed the souls of her mother and grandmother? Ruta's aura was tattered, her ability for discernment between herself and the outside world was riddled with holes. Her aura was like her mother's homeland; soil full of blood, shame and a yearning to be free.

Part of her was stuck in her parental genetic past and expectations of her present mind's eye. After several sessions of using Sunshine Wattle, the essence Waratah was needed. I muscle tested Ruta and she responded strongly to Waratah. Ian White prescribes this flower essence for people who are going through the darkest hour of their lives and are in utter despair. Ruta was at that level. She needed to have her survival skills and courage to cope brought forward. This essence has been proven to enhance and amplify those skills. I recommended that she take this bouquet for seven weeks.

Every week, the buzz in her head began to subside. Her ability to listen became "clean." This meant she was listening quietly without preconceived channeling. We all do preconceived channeling, listening half-heartedly, as we second-guess what a person is going to say. The flower essences helped dissipate her fears. Within the cavity of her heart was the fragile space necessary to truly listen.

After a year of coming for healing sessions, Ruta had created a balance between her interior and exterior life. She told me of times when she would sit in her kitchen nook, allowing the morning sun to bath her and her black cat Viva into tranquility. Viva would purr with contented gratitude.

Simmering in a green porcelain tea kettle was the tea, Maisytos Zoleliu Arbatos. The mixture filled the air with the smell of oregano, rowan fruit, red currants and a lemon peel. Ruta would sip the tea, then whisper the poetry of Kazys Bradunas, creating calmness on the water of her storm. Kazys Bradunas had started Zeme, the Lithuanian poetry movement with its distinct roots in the earth. Kazys Bradunas' poems grounded her, giving her a place to land during episodes of turmoil within her soul.

"But where does my home await me?
Far on the edge of the plains.
Ashes overgrown with grass."

Reading his poems helped Ruta to develop a sense of gratitude about where she lived. In the beginning it seemed that only Viva knew about gratitude, purring loudly in Ruta's lap, as she listened to her recite Bradunas's poems. During our sessions, I kept reminding Ruta that gratitude was an intentional choice. It wasn't the result of her purchase of a new kitchen tablecloth, or her accomplishment of losing three pounds and keeping it off. Her heart was opening and Ruta made the conscious choice to find gratitude all around her. Of course this was done with Viva's help.

The two were making spiritual progress thanks to the morning ritual of Ruta reading poetry from her mother's country and counting their blessings. During one of our sessions Ruta shyly told me she was "coming to her senses." It was through those senses that she was beginning to appreciate her world. "Yesterday, I made Juoda Duona Su Cesnakais." My eye brows jumped to attention. My mind knew what that meant. I stifled a gasp of desire for this Lithuanian delicacy. I kept my mouth closed, but my taste buds remembered the texture of the fried Lithuanian rye bread with garlic in my mouth. The twinkle in Ruta's eyes saved me, "I brought you some," she said.

"Thank God," I said, and almost made the sign of the cross. What an art form it was to fry the bread in oil to just the right point, crisp but not soggy. Ruta spoke of the Russian market in West Sacramento. The bread would arrive from Lithuania every Wednesday. It was a small hole in the wall grocery, invisible to the KGB that lingered in everyone's dreams. It was full of a thousand tasty memories of the homeland. Ruta loved that place, even though it was Russian. The bread would disappear by mid-morning. Only Lithuanian rye bread would make it perfect. Crushed garlic spread on top. Memories of this delicacy crafted a smile out of my lips, "I can wait till after the session to try some," I said, valiantly.

That was sort of a lie. It would take a lot of effort to keep my mind present in this room and not wonder off to Lithuania. "You are a dear." Gratitude comes in many forms.

CHAPTER THIRTEEN

"Living the Vision"

I have always been blessed with deep friendships; the kind that last a lifetime. Nitya Chaitanyanand was a good friend who always helped me find important things when I had lost them: my smile, perspective on a situation, and sometimes awareness. Her unique sense of historical view-point and Hindi courage was refreshing. She had the kind of courage that Krishna instilled in Arjuna, the central character of the ancient Indian epic Mahabharata and plays a key role in the Bhagavad Gita alongside Krishna.

It was Nitya, who would help me learn about the sixth chakra.

One summer California day, while doing paper work in the healing room, I started to rub the skin between my temples. Often an itch would start, just where a bindi would be placed if I were a Hindi woman. "The itch of the third eye," I would call it. The itch of awareness.

I got up from my desk and went to my cabinet, holding my client files. The sixth file cabinet had a solid clicking sound when you pressed the latch to open it. The drawer would glide open to reveal memories. It was the same click that the old metal Nikon made when I snapped a picture. This cabinet was full of clients' files who wanted to work on the misunderstood sixth chakra. This chakra was the source of insight, clairvoyance. It drew most of its energy from the brain and the seventh chakra. But what did insight mean? The words of Milarepa, one of Tibet's most famous yogis and poets, filled the room as I whispered his song:

"I see clearly that bliss is void of substance,
I see all things manifest without discriminating,
I see clearly that which is beyond all words
These are the three sights."

Pulling on the latch of the filing cabinet, again and again, the clicki-ty-clack propelled me into a memory of Nitya's beloved Goyandka family. Their green file folder was in the back. A,B,C, the alphabet was still a jumble of letters for my dyslexic mental frame of mind. The files were in order by mystery: unsolved, unfinished business. Eventually time would put the pieces together and the files could be moved closer to their correct alphabetical order.

I clicked the latch again, as if to induce a hypnotic trance of this memory.

The office was unbearably hot. It happened every August. The dry heat sucked the oxygen out of the air just as Nitya slammed the office door shut when she entered. She took two steps and curled into a half-fetal position on the floor, sobbing and rocking. "Krishna, Krishna," she cried in a mixture of Hindi and English that made no sense. There was a mixture of words and worlds, "Jai, Jai. Krishna, Krishna. They killed a good man. He did nothing." Now she held her palms up to the celling, as if holding the images of Sunder Goyandka and his wife Sita for all to see. "How can they bear the death of their son Jai? Krishna, Krishna."
"It shouldn't have happened. What kind of a place is this?"

There was nothing I could do. I put a Pashmina shawl over her body filled with sorrow and shame. It seemed fitting since Kashmir was one of her favorite places to visit and this shawl was made there. Pashmina is a fine wool. The finer textiles are still woven in Kashmir, India. Literally translated from Persian, Pashmina means "soft gold" and that is what I wanted to protect her with.

Even in this swelter, Nitya needed the protection of her culture and an infusion of gold. She continued to wail for what seemed like forever; each tear a thousand years, each droplet landing in the Sea of Samsara. Nothing could save her until she landed on the shore of her Guru's outstretched arms. So, I sat in silence and watched her body convulse, drifting into a deep sleep that would save her from consciousness.

An hour later, she woke and seemed ready for some Chai; hot, creamy, fragrant with black tea, fresh cardamom, cinnamon and enough sugar to bring up her blood sugar level.

"Thank you," she said, her outstretched right-hand trembling as she accepted the Chai in an orange ceramic tea cup. She took the cup and turned it clockwise so that her eyes were also filled with its orange color. "Orange, that is what Swamiji wears," she said, and bent her head as if to start another episode of wailing.

"Yes, Yes. Swamiji is with us always," I said and swirled my cupped left hand around her body and swiftly scooped the air around her. The energy surrounding her was propelled into the ground next to me. This action deflected her emotional energy of sorrow and let it be transmuted into the earth. Pointing to a comfortable lounge chair next to the massage table, I spoke softly, "Please, take this chair and keep covered." Her eyes were clear and black. She was focusing and gathering her thoughts in present time. She blinked to clear her mental sight, while simultaneously taking in mouthfuls of deep breaths.

"Ah cha." Nitya breathed out quietly.

Sita called me for prayers and let out the hell she and Sunder were living. "It must have been two weekends ago. Jai. You remember Jai? He was so tall. So handsome." For a moment, her mind carried her eyes up toward the celling again, searching for some lost photo album of his family. Her eyes searching for happy Kodak moments. "Jai grew…"

"That was the past tense. Where is he now?" Anger gushed through my teeth and the bile of intuition crept up into my throat. "Where is Jai now?"

"They killed him in his front yard. Right there. In front of his wife."

"Where were the children?" I gasped.

She covered her face with disbelief, her words creeping out of her mouth in a monotone fashion, "He's dead. They killed him."

"Here, here. Take this." I had jumped up and sprinted to my dispensary for flower essences. First, I doused my mouth with the Bach Flower emergency essence and then put in four drops of the Bach Flower Emergency essence and five drops of Waratah in a glass of water for her. "Drink this. Forget the tea." I took the tea cup from her hand. "Can you start from the beginning?"

"Ah cha. Krishna, Krishna." She was pulling strength from Krishna while I sat silently waiting for her to gather words in English. Then with two huge gulps, Nitya twirled the shawl in the air and wrapped it around her bowed shoulders to secure her energy field. "Sita called the next morning after it happened. It was Sunday. Jai had worked all day Saturday. Sita said he had been working six days a week for the past three months." Nitya twirled her hands in a circle that seemed to circumvent God's earth of human toil. "Sita said he was playing with the children in the living room and drinking beer. He was loud and his laughter was crazy. They had fought earlier that morning. She was mad. He was mad. Exhausted. They fought a lot lately." Nitya stopped abruptly and pulled the shawl tighter around her shoulders, protecting her heart. "Mae called the police. She was frightened of his anger. When the police arrived, they heard them screaming in Hindi. It was Kali. The fury of Kali, Sita said." Nitya gulped a bucket of air and continued, "They wanted him out of the house. One officer took Mae to the police car, the second officer ran into the house to be with the children. A third took out his gun pointing it at Jai as he came out of the house. Were these men Parashram? Kali Kali."

Nitya was out of breath. She was beginning to pant like a dog. Her eyes turned midnight black. I took her hand and placed it around the glass of flower essence water. "Drink. Drink more."

She threw herself back into the rocker after gulping the water. Her nostrils flared as she began reciting a mantra from Kali Ma, as if it might change what was to come, "Pracanda-canda-mundayor maha-balai-ka-khandini." Nitya was beginning to take in small sips of air. "May Kali take away all sins." Her forehead had a shine and she began to glow. Nitya was working herself into a trance.

"No, No. Come back." I stroked her arm. Hoping the touch would alert her to present time. She turned and focused her gaze on me. She frowned at what she saw. "You are not Indra!"

"Come back Nitya. Don't flip out on me. Next. What happened next," I demanded.

"They told him to kneel and put his hands behind his back. Mae started to scream from the police car. Kneeling, Jai jerked his right arm for some reason. It was just enough reason for a reaction. A nanosecond, and the decision was made. The officer shot him. Just shot him dead." She could say no more. Covering her head with her shawl, she wept. I looked down at her and realized, she was too tired to feel, too sad to morn, too weak to comprehend.

A month later I called Sita and Sunder to offer my condolences. I wandered in disbelief for the longest time before calling Sita. Nitya was a wreck and I was in no better shape. The office was closed from the shock of life.

"Sita, this is Laima. I've called to offer my...,"

She started whispering softly, as if not to wake the young boy Jai in her head. "Can you come over this afternoon for tea? I have something I need to show you." Her voice shifted, leaving a feeling of pride in between her tears, "You know these things. Come at four."

"Of course, certainly." It wasn't anything I had expected. This all reminded me of the meeting with the owl going back to my tent at the first dance Joseph had led. That owl was full of knowing. Hair stood up on the back of my neck; goose bumps were sprinkled up and down my arms; while visions of Jai as a boy danced in my head, "Of course I'll come at four."

CHAPTER FOURTEEN

"Knowing Your Truth"

When Sita opened the front door to their house, she looked thinner, but there was an odd radiance about her. The words from the Tulasi Ramayana came to mind about the Devi Sita: "Offer your reverence to Rama's beloved Sita, the source of the world's creation, and destruction. Sita the Devi who removes all miseries and is the bringer of all auspicious gifts."

Sita opened the door wider and smiled, with a touch of sadness in her left eye. "Come in, come in." She grabbed both of my hands and pressed them together, as if to instruct me on how to pray. Smiling, she placed my folded hands on her forehead. Letting go of my hands, she bowed and adjusted her shawl. "Come. Let's go into the dining room."

"Tea." It wasn't a question of asking did I want tea. It was a statement of what came next. "Last week, I was able to go into Jai's room. We hadn't moved anything since he got married. In a different time, Mae would be here. Helping us. But it is different now." She expelled a big, expansive breath, one that blew from the Indian Ocean to the bay of San Francisco. "At cha." Sita was at the age where home mattered. Not all her relatives had moved to America. The young ones seemed to zip back and forth from Delhi to San Francisco, as if a mere small cosmic bridge separated the family. "At cha. You know how he loved to make chai for you."

I glanced at the living room table where the tea set was placed. Next to it was a folded notebook, with drawing paper inside. Sita touched the notebook, and then began to pour the tea. It seemed like a lifetime before our formal conversation stopped and she picked up a neatly folded paper from the notebook; turning it around in her hands.

I found this in one of Jai's art boxes. It is a drawing. He even signed and dated it. Let's see." She touched her right forefinger to her Ajna. Her gesture reminded me that in the Western culture; the Ajna, was the third eye, located between the eyebrows at the bridge of the nose. This center is located directly in front of the pineal gland. For Sita the Ajna is a sacred spot where she applied a bindi to show respect for this chakra. This afternoon, Sita had applied a bright, emerald bindi on top of her third eye. Touching it, the bindi seemed to glow. "Let's see." She repeated herself and drew out the "e" vowel. "He would have been… Thirteen. Yes, thirteen. Coming into puberty." Her smile glowed. That concerned me. "Jai liked art." She handed me the folded paper.

When I unfolded it, my eyes were taken into a moment from the not so distant past.

"Yes, that is exactly the way it was," Sita sighed, "When Mae saw the drawing, she became hysterical. Sunder wept openly for the first time since his father died, He kept saying in Hindi, "How did he know? How did he know?" In front of me was the exact moment of Jai's death. It was sketched in pencil, every detail was exact. The police car with a female figure inside; a young man kneeling with his hands behind his back, a policeman behind him with a smoking gun, two small children on the porch of a house. It was just as Nitya had described it to me in my office.

Sita touched my hand, pulling me out of the scene that had been created fifteen years earlier. "He knew. At cha," Sita let the words out of her mouth with a sigh. "Jai had said he knew when he was going to die. But I made nothing of it. You know our culture. Past lives. Living again. So. Young boys, they say many things."

I stared at the pencil drawing again and was thankful to be sitting down. It was the first example I had seen of future sight, which is activated by the third eye. "I thought this might help you. With what you practice and all you know." She touched my hand. "His death was not for nothing. This will help you understand the mystery. " She sighed again. "You will learn from him. Yes." She leaned over to look into my eyes, to see if I was comprehending any of this.

"Yes." I mumbled, with no comprehension at all.

Anger and rage were my bedfellows from that day on. This wasn't supposed to happen; how did he know? There was a bitter taste in my mouth. How could it be? I had started my journey of spiritual growth wanting to know the truth. In my Kiva Journal, the introduction began:

"What I have to tell you is the whole truth and nothing but the truth. Actually, that is a lie. If you grew up in the sixties believing that the camera never lied, and truth could be ferreted out by a good journalist from Columbia University, the first sentence can't be true. Then the "truth" was a known factor, able to be tested, quantified and analyzed. The truth rode on the back of facts. Every genuine piece of journalism was based on facts and that is how we knew reality."

Now when I look back on those days, I call that journalistic truth: "Colombian Truth." Not unlike the drug, sweet to the taste until reality sets in. But that isn't the case in the 90s: Schrodinger, Einstein, even Bailey; they all helped to create a New Age.

Now there are facts and the truth resides in our individual perception.

Let me start over. I have my life experience, my truth and I would like to share that reality with you. It all happened and that's the simple truth." I deeply wanted to share my spiritual truth.

I will carry that picture in my mind's eye for ever. Several days later, wanting to see no one, I started rummaging through my black seven drawer cabinet again. It was late evening, between ten and eleven. I often came in there to read; allowing my mind to drift and sail away, with no physical interruptions. Names had always alluded me and this heat filled the night air, I was trying to remember a teacher of mine. Then finally I remembered his name: Walter Makichen. I had taken a class from him on the topic of chakras. What was it that he said about the 6th chakra? I looked for his tapes I had bought: The Hidden You, A Journey Into the Human Energy System: The Chakras.

I couldn't find them.

Smiling with a mouthful of sarcasm, I walked to my desk. I was looking for intellectual comfort, my ego was frightened. So I picked up papers, turned over piles of files, ran my fingers across rows of spiritual books. In a drawer, I found some lecture notes under "truth," not the 6th chakra or author's name. "Full circle," I whispered to myself. I was reminded of my mother's Estonian saying, "A circle is round."

"This is the chakra where we could see true meaning. Truth." Printed with a black Sharpie on a 4x6 lined note card, the "T" was capitalized and underlined. "With this chakra open, we can pick things apart. It is a chakra that wants to know the deeper truth, not just what's on the surface. When stimulated, this chakra could arouse the intellect, so the witness could understand the many layers of "truth." Nitya had once told me her Guru had said, "There is only one Truth, but we see many truths. As long as we see many Truths, liberation cannot happen. Seeing only one Truth is waking up. This one Truth is called Oneness or non-duality. In Oneness who is the seer and who is the seen?"

I sat in the lounge chair and threw some of my note cards in the air, watching them scatter, fall and land, filling the four directions. I challenged them, as if they might be soldiers of good knowledge, guarding some hidden treasury. "Who are you?" I asked, pleading with them, "We have spent the last thousand years naming everything. Scientifically, cataloging, weighing. That is how I know you. You have a name. No name, nothing." I snapped my fingers, "Nothing. You are paper, nothing without my writing. My words."

And then the voice of Makichen came to me from his lecture, "The 6th chakra reveals just what is. It is a chakra that gives you a clear imprint of what is around you. Nothing more."

Nitya said the same, "If you develop your witness, the truth will be revealed. This chakra has the capacity to see patterns. With the observer, things and people are revealed."

I was stymied. "What do you mean reveal?"

"We have to accept what IS, not though our karmic lenses. New. Fresh." Her voice nudged me to listen, "Your Eurocentric world. There is safety in naming. Yes! We project a name onto things and people rather than having them reveal themselves." I could see Nitya's hands swirling in the air, forming letters. "What kind of a world do you need to project in order to survive? Did your parent's land here to be saved? From what? Is your American white culture the best?" She was talking to someone else, it couldn't be me. I needed to stop this conversation in my head.

"Snap out of it, Laima," I was embarrassed, remembering that encounter with Nitya. Something she said was right and I didn't like it.

"Wouldn't it be hell if I had to look at you anew each time we met? A hellish Ground Hog's Day every day." I was overwhelmed by the thought. I knew Nitya and she knew me. I leaned over and picked up a note card from the floor. "For most people Karma equals past knowledge, determines what they see." In bold Sharpie letters I had written: "to learn means you don't know." I picked up the note card and put it to my fore head, remembering the Johnny Carson Show and Ed McMahon. "What is this process to weigh the evidence, dissect, take it apart, look deeply?" Flipping the card toward the ceiling, "Here's Johnny!"

"What was I so scared of? What did I need to control? What if 'it' was different than me?" That was problem, I wanted everything to be the same. White. No colors. Different was hard. America was hard. My parents wanted to fit in. They didn't know the rules and how to fit in. I didn't know what was the American truth." My body began to curl up in the chair, my knees touched my chin. Trying for a fetal position, my body started rocking. Rocking like the ocean. Feeling the never-ending rocking as we came over on the boat."

"All new." I whispered, as tears dripped down my face and fell onto the floor filled with note cards. "All new."

CHAPTER FIFTEEN

"Both Are Healed"

For about three months afterwards, I couldn't drop into a deep sleep. Tossing and turning, thinking surely, I would die. And something did die. The American dream.

If Nitya brought bad news, more than often she brought good news. It was a Monday morning, with the sky bearing the gift of another sunny California day. Nitya arrived at my office door.

"I want you to meet someone," she said.

He stood in the door way, reluctant to step over the threshold and come into my office. Shannon looked everywhere, except into my eyes. He wore khaki shorts and light blue t-shirt, which exposed his sensitive pink skin. His disheveled red hair glowed as he kept wringing his chapped, dry hands together.

"Come in. Both of you. Come in, Shannon." I was careful not to look at him directly. He was shy and autistic. Stopping in the middle of the room, he shrugged his shoulders and smiled.

"I have to wash my hands. Where is the bathroom?" he asked.

"To your left." When he was there and had closed the door, I looked at Nitya, inquisitively. I gestured to her, the universal "What's up?" sign, with palms pointing to the heavens.

"He's here to help you get out of your funk. He sees things differently. You might be interested." Nitya's left and right eye brows shot up, forming the familiar McDonald's Arches. A wry smile crossed her face.

"He also has a synesthetic brain. His third eye is completely open. All data that he perceives is taken in and multiplied. One sense stimulates another. You know." She was tiring of my blank face. "Taste numbers, see color around people. No judgment. Just a world totally different from yours." She covered her mouth to hide a snicker. "Shannon, are you finished in there?" she called to him through the bathroom door.

"Almost." His voice was hesitant. "It smells like avocados in here."

"That's all right, dear. Finish up and come out."

One wall of the bathroom had been painted green. In fact, Williams Paint Company labeled that green: California Avocado.

Shannon came out licking his lips and smiling, "I like your bathroom, it tastes likes avocados." He wrung his half-dried hands together.

And so it was, Shannon began to guide me into a world I couldn't perceive, but was willing to explore with his help.

By the next time we met, I had read a great deal about the synesthetic mind. The word synesthesia means the union of the senses. It is a brain condition that links a person's senses together. People with this condition have more neural cross talk. The stimulation of one sense automatically stimulates other senses. The neurons that fire for sight can activate smell or sound. It is estimated that four per cent of our world population has synesthetic abilities. In the mind of Duke Ellington, "a D note looked like dark blue burlap, a G note light blue satin." David Hockney and Joan Mitchell have synesthesian.

Shannon and I began to explore our separate worlds. They were linked by our love to explore. "Shannon, what was the first word you spoke?"

"Yellow. It was the sunflower, yellow." He smiled and it was infectious. "It made my mother very happy. I was three years old. Yellow."

We often shared lunch at McDonald's. The culinary questions were: "Does a Big Mac feel pointy or round inside your mouth? When you look at the yellow brownish color of the walls at our booth, do you taste french-fries?"

Some afternoons, we would just lie on the grass in front of my house and look at the sky, which was never blue in his eyes. The shapes of clouds would sometimes gag him from their smell. I did see an elephant once in those puffy cumulus clouds.

The synapse of joy, forever clicking in our shared consciousness, helped me heal in many ways.

CHAPTER SIXTEEN

"Seven Times Seven"

In the fall, I started working with Dotty Shaffer. Her file was in the last drawer of the black file cabinet marked in bold blue magic marker: seventh chakra.

Dotty was a character out of her own romance novel, living forever in the pages of Architectural Digest. She was known as the best interior designer in Northern California. Sacramento Magazine had just done a feature article on her. The photography was gorgeous. Million dollar homes in Sacramento and Davis, decorated in themes that were wild, exacting and only Dotty could pull that off. What I mean about exacting is every detail was perfect and historically correct. Dotty had traveled to the Roy Rogers estate to get some ideas for a western theme in the Capay Valley. She turned that mansion into a Western museum and the senator loved it.

As for her own home, things were not so perfect.

"I've tried everything. It's a mess. Not just some of the rooms. Every-thing. I can't bring anyone over for fear that they would see the real me. I have paid dearly for an organizing specialist; I've had the house Feng Shui-ed; a friend's uncle who is Native American came over to do a cleansing ceremony. I gagged on the burning sage. Didn't do a thing. I've fired three personal secretaries who couldn't keep me and my house organized. Hell, in Georgia, I even sold a house I was living in which was filled to the brim. Just walked away with everything in it. It was just too cluttered. What's going on with me?"

"Here drink this," I said, using my standby prescription: four drops of Bach Flower remedy named Emergency. I dispensed it like regular doctors prescribed antibiotics. "This will calm you." And it did.

"You are the last resort," she gasped.

"I usually am," I sighed.

While she was talking, a little voice in my head kept whispering, "Seventh Chakra. She's a seventh chakra girl."

I tilted my head a little to see if I could get a glimmering of her aura. Nope. I did not have the ability to see auras. But the voice inside was still persistent. "Wide open seventh chakra. Clear as day."

"Do you wear hats?" I smiled cautiously. It threw her off balance.

"What?" Dotty touched her head, as if to check.

"Do you wear hats?" I repeated.

"I love them. But I never wear them. My head's too big." Dotty brushed her dyed blond hair behind her left ear.

I didn't know where to start. So I suggested a Reiki session to relax her body and mind, while I was figuring out how to describe her dilemma in layman's terms.

The seventh chakra is at the top of the head. Most new age reading material will tell you that violet is the color for the crown chakra. Violet can offer a person a sense of wholeness, completion of a process. Violet can connect with inner sadness and the process of letting go. Being an interior designer, Dotty could relate to the color violet. She loved the color and used it a lot with her clients. Violet people, who have a smooth-running chakra system, are open-minded, curious and deep thinkers. On the physical level, this chakra is associated with the pituitary gland, which regulates the endocrine system.

Where the sixth chakra can dissect situations and has the ability to judge, categorize and name different events, the seventh chakra holds our basic truths from our past lives and rarely can we change them. From the seventh chakra comes the saying, "If you believe it, you can do it." It is the chakra that lets in universal energy, so that karmic learning can be processed in this lifetime. The personality that has an open seventh chakra can have a hard time making decisions, because anything goes. It is a person who has a diverse set of friends and loves to eat all kinds of food. Variety is the spice of life.

Dotty had decorated every room in her house in a different theme: Western kitchen, Oriental Zen living room that needed de-cluttering badly, Savannah bedroom, what she hadn't decided was where: Savannah, Georgia or the Savannah in Africa. There were two water buffalo heads in the hall way, awaiting her decision. The half-painted laundry room came off of the master bedroom, which still had boxes from her Georgia home. The guest room was literally boxed in. It went on and on. The garage could only hold two cars and Dotty had three. She bought everything and couldn't give up anything. To let go of something would mean making a decision. They all had the same value. Wonderful! Dotty had a way of seeing wonderment in nearly all objects. It was all too traumatizing to make a decision. She was a miracle worker for others. In her own life, there was only disaster.

Lavender kept coming up in our Reiki sessions. After one of our sessions, when the heat had died down, I walked back to my office. I leafed through Ian White's book, Bush Flower Essences. The quote by Samuel Smiles jumped out at me. "The shortest way to do many things is to do only one thing at once." Ian White had used the quote to introduce Jacaranda mimosaefolia, which translated into everyday English as Jacaranda. It is a tree growing on the East Coast of Australia. The flowers of this tree are a bright lavender. Dotty would have approved had she known anything about flower essences. Ian had concluded that the Jacaranda was a flower essence for "ditherers." It was a flower essence for people who could start but couldn't stop projects and making decisions. The second ingredient for this bouquet came from the Paw Paw flower. This white flower grows on an evergreen tree originating in Mexico. Ian White suggested that this was an excellent remedy for activating awareness of the Higher Self. What I wanted from Dotty was to develop a global sense of herself. I had projected that her heightened awareness would lead to a greater ability to focus in her everyday activities.

Within a month, Dotty was much more focused. She had found Tanner, a young college student who went to the Art Institute in Sacramento. Tanner became her right-hand man. She eased into deciding what to keep, what to give way and a set of goals were labeled "NOW one at a time" on a lavender folder, on top her mahogany writing table.

As a thank you, Dotty took me shopping for hats. "It's interesting," she mused, "twirling her straw blond hair, "Now I wear a hat when I feel flighty. It feels like my head just popped open. A cold draft comes around my shoulders." She shivered at the thought. "You need some more hats," she said to me.

"I need a new cowboy hat."

"You want to sell your Stetson, the one that Ray Bradbury signed? I'd love to buy it!" Dotty knew a treasure when she saw it.

For a moment, my mind flew to New Mexico, where a Sun Moon Dance was being held. That was where I met Ray Bradbury with his graying hair in a dust-covered bookstore that was next to a health food store. I am sure I would have missed seeing him had it not been for the pre-dance jitters. This Sun Moon dance created by Joseph was being held in the desert. The desert, which meant: 110 Fahrenheit, no cloud cover, dust, and dried cattle bones everywhere. It was imperative we had clean bodies to survive this grueling encounter. All the dancers were obsessed with getting the junk out of our bodies before the dance. Sluggish toxic bodies equal sluggish, hellish dance. So, there we were in the shopping center ready to go into the health food store to find detoxing everything when the bookstore caught my eye.

Stopping in seemed logical. Feed the mind, feed the body. My father loved books and I followed the genetic suit. I couldn't pass it by. Bookstores were like garage sales; you never knew what you would find. What treasures lie in a weathered brown box on the lawn or down the bookstore aisle marked "Fiction/ no drinks PLEASE". It was an open, airy store, featuring the writer Ray Bradbury. It was a book signing for his one work of science fiction Fahrenheit 451. "How appropriate," I thought to myself, "it's 100 degrees in the shade and paper ignites at 451 Fahrenheit." I was wearing khaki shorts, a white t-shirt and a four-beaver pelt, Stetson cowboy hat. Taking it off, I reached inside my pocket and pulled out a flowered bandana, my mother had worn while gardening and wiped the sweat off the inside band of the Stetson.

Upon reflection, I don't know what possessed me to meet Bradbury and tell him about the dance. I never talked to strangers about my work with Joseph. When I have tried in the past, people would shake their heads and look perplexed - not in their realm of experience; their minds couldn't stretch that far. Most people don't explore, whether in their minds or in this world. But Ray Bradbury looked up, leaned back in his chair and adjusted his thick glasses to somehow hear better. We talked about the Tewa culture, the power of observation and the dance coming up.

"You live what I write about. Take me with you." And he pointed to my Stetson. I gave him the hat and inside he wrote: Ray Bradbury is with you. NOW! 4/4/91.

It would take many years before I would begin to understand our relationship and the affect he had on my crown chakra.

Joseph once told me that what you wore on or around your crown chakra, was a manifestation of your higher self.

I shook my body and returned to present time. "No, I need to wear that one a bit longer." I winked at her and she did a 180 degree turn around, as if to show off her body. I titled my head to take in the length of her frame.

"You've been doing those yoga exercises I suggested from Cajzoran Ali. Haven't you!"

"Yes, I have and glad you noticed. I am much more limber. But, they are hard to do if you have to concentrate on that breathing." She emphasized the word that, as if "that" referred to some esoteric process called breathing. It really wasn't part of her healthy repertoire. Breathing, that is.

She twirled her body again. "And where did you get that skinny, blue book by Cajzoran Ali? Who would ever read, Divine Posture Influences upon Endocrine Glands . The title is as long as the book. Those God-awful pictures. What were they doing in the twenties?" She stood up straight, putting more pressure on her feet to exaggerate their muscular development. "No matter, I keep doing those yoga poses, like you said."

I smiled broadly at Dotty and she let go of my energy field, so she could meander off to another aisle of clothing. Standing still, I tried to visualize the cover picture of Cajzoran Ali wrapped in white. The caption under the photo read: "Originator and true exponent of Divine Postures."

If the seventh chakra had a connection with the endocrine glands, this tiny book was a treasure trove of yoga postures to strengthen and keep the universal energy flowing through that system. It wasn't by chance that Dotty was now focused and looking like her million-dollar clients.

CHAPTER SEVENTEEN

"The Art of Dying"

No matter how good a healer you are, you are never prepared for witnessing the transition of a loved one. The call that Marquerite, my youngest sister, was being taken to the hospital stunned me. She had pancreatic cancer. It was too painful for her to be on the farm anymore and Lee, our middle sister, couldn't take care of her. Marquerite needed hospice.

So, I was on the road to Michigan.

Driving is a psychic drug. Like any good American, I was addicted. Driving has always comforted me. I feel in control. My mind can safely wander while my body and cognitive brain are engaged in a relatively mundane activity.

The Michigan landscape blurred from gray into asphalt black, as I raced toward Lansing, Michigan. The Jamestown Hospital parking lot was relatively empty when I arrived. Three spot lights on the west wall of the hospital pointed to the red painted emergency entrance doors. After midnight, that was the only way visitors could enter.

All hospitals have the same smell of decay and bleach. I hated that smell. Intermittently, I held my breath and looked at room numbers. Finding Marguerite's room was relatively easy; entering it was hard. Cupped in her Slenderella thin fingers was a call button twinkling on and off, on and off, on off. For a moment, I was mesmerized by its blinking light. As the oldest of three, I always had to be brave. "Go on in and look her in the face," I said to myself. Bravery with family matters came naturally. But now, too much had happened. I couldn't do it. Clutching my bag, I entered and shuffled toward the window. Placing my brown canvas bag on the window heating vent, the idea of essential oils saved me from wanting to cry. Searching the bottom of my purse, I grabbed the eight-ounce bottle marked "peace and calming." I had worked with the Young Living Essential oils for several years now. I passed the bottle under my nose, the smell relaxed me completely. All at once, the bottle had a life of its own and jumped out of my right hand onto the grated heating vent. The contents oozed onto it. The aroma began to fill the room.

"Dear God, what have I done?" I chastised myself under my breath.

A nurse popped her head into the room. "Excuse me, Miss. Are you a relative?"

I turned sideways, trying to hide the accident I had created, "Yes, she's my sister."

"Oh! She is on a morphine drip. It's late and she'll be sleeping for a long while."

The nurse's smile gave me reason to stop, sit down and relax in the chair a few feet from Marguerite.

"My name is Madeline," said the woman as she entered the room. "I am one of the night nurses. I didn't realize how tired I was." Madeline turned her torso to stretch, just as Mary, an intensive care nurse sauntered into the room.

"On a break?" Mary asked Madeline.

"Yes, I need it." said Madeline. "I thought you were on vacation. Mine's coming up next week. Couldn't come any sooner."

The door opened and Jeffery who was six feet two and all muscle stood surveying the room. "Hmmmm, Jeffery, come here," said Madeline, her voice thick with sleepiness. "Did you make coffee yet?"

Jeffery was all teddy bear; every word he spoke had the sound of human kindness in it, except for now, "It's not my turn; it's her turn," he said, indicating Michelle who was standing behind him. "Ya' know, every time I'm on a shift with her, I end up doing her work. By the way, did she ever fill out those SB4 forms?" Jeffery stepped into the room and suddenly began smiling something as Michelle took his place at the door.

"Michelle what are you doing down here? Come ooo onnnn in here," said Mary, as she stretched out the word "on" as far as her voice could carry it and then wrapped her own arms around her chest, as if holding a baby. Mary, I soon realized, liked to badger her fellow nurses. Twenty years of hospital service gave this Italian grandmother the right and privilege to do so. Her smiling mouth displayed two gold fillings; it was the same gold that apparently filled her heart.

"Don't you go badgering me. We all need a break," said Michelle, who stepped in and stood close to Jeffery, who by now was standing by the window, with a euphoric smile on his face.

As each person entered the room, I moved to the left, closer to Marguerite's bed. With each step closer to Marguerite, the thought crossed my mind that if any more people came into the room, I would have to crawl in bed with her to make more space for everyone. We were a very accommodating family, but this was ridiculous. The party atmosphere was beginning to unnerve me. After all, my sister was dying of cancer; this was not a staff lounge.

Mary tightened her grip on herself in order to push her words out, "Michelle, Michelle! What are you gonna do with that girlfriend of yours?" All eyes shifted to Michelle as her eyebrows curved into a question mark. But the twinkle in her eye told us she knew exactly what to say, "Well," she said, trying to imitate Mary's cadence. "I just might maarrrrry her."

A hum of approval filled the air. "Yes, indeedy, you should do that!"

Mary loved to attend weddings.

Everyone agreed, because, suddenly, everyone wanted a reason to celebrate life. By now I was ready to have a psychotic break. My island of despair had shifted into a scene out of My Greek Wedding. It seemed like any minute party favors were going to be handed out, until I was saved by Nurse Ratchet, who was built like a tank. The minute she walked in the room, it was clear, she didn't allow anyone to cross into her territory without her knowing it. Germany would have won World War II, if she had been around then. Instead, her grandparents had come to find new opportunities after the First Great War.

"What is going on here?" she asked, immediately transporting everyone to Auschwitz.

I had, it seemed, been saved by Göring, Hitler's favorite henchman. What a karmic turnaround! "Michelle, Jeffery!" Nurse Ratchet said, and stamped her left foot as if grinding their names into the ground. "Who is down below in intensive care? What are you all doing in here?" Nostrils flaring, she took one giant breath and then suddenly smiled. Her smile momentarily stunned everyone. That expression had apparently not crossed her face since eighth grade. No one on the staff had ever seen her do that. That's when I realized that the oozing Young Living Essential oils I'd spilled all over the radiator had induced the relaxed state to anyone who encountered the smell in Marguerite's room. Like a screen that popped before my mind I could see the odor had triggered a memory of Nurse Ratchet's 13th birthday party, when her Uncle Thomas surprised her with a puppy, and she had smiled the whole day.

"Well, you better go back," said Nurse Ratchet, as she leaned against the door, inhaling the memory of that September day forty years ago and the puppy she grew to love. Bowing respectfully, as if witnessing the aftermath of a miracle, everyone left the room, except the nurse assigned to my sister.

"That was odd. I have never seen her smile before," said Madeline aloud, as she re-entered the now quiet room. A calmness still consumed the room, even in its emptiness, allowing me to sit down and bravely hold my sister's hand. Like an owl on the evening hunt, my mind reviewed the last twenty minutes. Was it really the oil that fell into the radiator that drew all those people into this room, that made them all so relaxed? As a Buddha smile came over my face, I knew that was it. It was like a giant diffuser radiating the Peace and Calming oil from Young Living, bringing with it a healing wave of human compassion.

Looking over at Marquerite, I realized she was finally experiencing something she had always wanted: the birthing process. But rather than a child, it was cancer. Each day it was growing bigger and bigger inside her. She reminded me of those mothers on the street. Pink cheeks, with watermelon tummies, that was Marquerite. The pain killers had given her an iridescent glow while she was sleeping. But when she woke, during her lucid moments, she pulled her nightgown over her belly, trying to hide the "thing" growing inside her body.

The next morning, Madeline pulled me aside, "These doctors here, they don't know about pain management. They know how to cut things out. But how to make a dying person comfortable, that's not their forte." Her eyes darted over to Marquerite. "Maybe it's time for Hospice. Social workers and Human Resources are on the third floor."

Marquerite's case worker was Mrs. Shaham. Her body was twenty years my junior, her eyes were twenty years my senior. I felt it was a good sign that a Hindi would help my sister to get to her next step - her soul's healing process. I had heard that this religion honored the concept of past lives. Marguerite felt she had remembered several past lives.

Mrs. Shaham waved me into her office, "This is my Taj Mahal" It was a cramped square room, filled with paperwork, that showed an exacerbated case load. "Please come in, sit." After sitting, Mrs. Shaham clutched Marguerite's paperwork to her heart. "Your sister has thirty days in hospice. That is what her insurance provides for. Just thirty days."

I gasped. I knew no one could predict the process of death. Would she live longer than thirty days?

"God will decide." She touched her right forefinger where she would have placed a bindi.

I leaned forward, our noses almost touching over the sea of papers. "Then what?" I whispered. "I have no money to keep her there, if she doesn't die in the prescribed thirty days, surely the ride back to the farm will kill her." For a moment a cold cynical voice echoed inside, "That is the objective, isn't it?"

Mrs. Shaham looked deeply into my eyes and smiled; as if she knew the gate keeper very well. "As you can see, my office is filled with paperwork. This is the red tape of samsara. Whatever time she will need, I am sure God will give it to her."

I sat back and let out a sigh of relief.

"Let us take it one day at a time. Yes! I will arrange for her transfer to the Hospice. Maybe you know of the Devi Durga? Ms. Laima? Marquerite will be going to Michigan's finest hospice. It is right here in Lansing. We are very proud of it." Mrs. Shaham pointed upward with her index finger, while her head swayed left to right. She reached for a small bottle of sandalwood oil that was on her bookshelf. "Here, place a few drops behind your ears and breath in deeply." I smiled and followed her instructions. "It comes from Hardwar, my Guru is there. Swami Paramanand Ji Maharaj. I can see by your face that you have not heard of him. The sandalwood, smells good? Yes?" She stood up and found some forms that needed to be completed before Marguerite could be taken to Hospice.

The paperwork went as smoothly as the ride to hospice. Marquerite was taken by ambulance, wrapped in morphine and an extra blue blanket. With all the drugs she was given, I didn't see much of a future for quality conscious time and that depressed me.

That night, I went to a local grocery store to safely wander in a daze. I didn't want to be conscious. Large discount stores always overwhelmed me. There I was on aisle sixteen whispering, "So many choices: brown rice pasta, gourmet egg noodles, wheat pasta, spinach pasta, rice pasta, pasta." I came to my senses in front of the "Summer FUN SALE" for CDs: The Night & Day Big Band, Country Western, Beach Boys, Jazz to Cool the Heat, on and on.

Driving home, Country Western music carried me out of my body and the words soothed unbearable thoughts. "Younger sisters aren't supposed to die before you. That's the rule. Isn't it?"

The next day, I drove to hospital and then remembered I should be at the Lansing Hospice. So, I turned the car around and drove to Lansing Hospice. The small hospice entranceway overflowed with flowers. The smell of different bouquets drifted down the right-hand hall where a row of eight private rooms faced each other. The left-hand hall opened to a specious waiting room, which had a kitchenette and a large dining room table.

Mrs. Kramer, the hospice nurse came up beside me. "Ms. Druskis. Your sister came in last night. It was an easy transition and we changed her medication. I have her records right here." She tapped the manila folder with her left hand. I could see that Mrs. Kramer loved this work and that comforted me, it was in her eyes. I was not looking forward to seeing my sister in her vegetative state, no matter how nice the setting. The nurse slipped her right hand under my elbow and guided me into Marquerite's room.

"Sherbet for everyone!" it was a queenly demand, as if the whole kingdom around her were receiving Krugerrands from the king's chest for their loyal support. I closed my eyes.

Then I blinked and blinked again. "Wrong room."

Mrs. Kramer shifted her right hand from my elbow to the small of my back and pushed me into the room. "Here we are."

Marquerite turned from the attention of her entourage to make her demands graciously understood to those entering, "Sherbet for everyone!" Everyone raised their cups of orange sherbet in unison and turned to me, "Here, Laima, this is for you."

Who were these people and why wasn't my sister dead? I smiled broadly and went blank inside. Marquerite was conscious, clear of mind and smiling. With the right combination of drugs, there was the illusion that she would get well.

For the first week in hospice, it was amazing her desire to learn. In the late afternoon, when her body was so tired, she asked me to read from Marko Pogacnik's book, Nature Spirits & Elemental Beings. To Marquerite and the author, "elemental beings" actually existed and there was an intelligence in the earth, nature, in everything.

My sister, Lee, and I placed pictures of her beautiful garden around the room. People used to come from all over Indiana to see her garden and bird sanctuary. Many people had never seen a Kiwi Tree, let alone its fruit. Marquerite loved watching the children who came with their parents. She shyly enjoyed the interaction between mother and daughters. Marquerite could not have children of her own. The garden was her child. It was ever-growing and changing.

One afternoon she read to me from her diary about the experience of her garden. "When the world was very young and we were an emerging species, perception was a blended rainbow. A woman in an open field of flowers might wonder what it would be like to be that flower. Her own consciousness would mix and flow into the flower. She would have a direct experience of the flower. She and the flower became one. I have that ability to quiet myself and become one with my garden. I am the garden of life."

I looked at her and thought of some of the research I had read in the past years, "Biologically, data gathered by our senses can be stored in the chromosomes, strung together in a certain format. This could be conceived of as a direct experience for the body." I thought for a moment, "Direct experience does not involve images or words, but is a free flow of direct cognitive material. We just have to be aware and consciously experience." I now knew that Marguerite did that often.

"Yes." Marguerite sighed, "Like being in our mother's womb. We have a direct experience of mom. I also have that experience when I am working in the garden or just sitting there meditating."

That afternoon I went home to nap, to forget that she was dying and that I really didn't know this extraordinary person. By now the road between Lee's house and the hospice became two exacting points: at one point, Marguerite was learning to leave her body forever and I was developing the skill of being present in my body.

Within the second week, Marguerite was becoming agitated in the morning as well as the afternoon. Fitting into her body seemed to be a hard chore, as she consciously woke up each morning or after a nap. When I came into the room this morning, she reached out her frail hand to hold mine, "It's so uncomfortable entering a dying body to be here with you all. I remember my etheric body hitting the wall and then trying to fit into this body. This dying body." Her voice was raspy.

"Stop, let me put the lip balm on. Don't talk." My fingers gently put the balm over her lips.

"I need water. I need water. I could feel coming into my body. Head First." She paused and licked her lips. "Instead of feet first. Remember how hard parking Dad's car. Para…. parallel parking was so hard. Remember!" Her lips cracked a smile.

She did remember well. For the first time, I realized that she was my teacher preparing me for my exit. She had learned about: chakras, meditation, becoming a vegetarian, the etheric body before she was twelve.

That night, Marquerite whispered, "Call Reverend Sally Perry. Please." Sally had worked with hundreds of people who were "passing over to the other side." Marguerite was caught in a Bardo of fear. Wanting to get out. But how? She wanted the help of this great healer, Sally Perry. "Get Sally Perry on the phone!"

"I am glad I can be here for you." Sally's voice was a little husky after climbing down the stairs. Entering her prayer room to light candles, she cradled her teal cordless phone with her right shoulder. Clearing her throat, Sally started her prayer:
"Grandmothers and Grandfathers of the East,
We call you in for the healing of Marguerite's mind.
We thank you for shattering old mind sets
 that do not serve her, Into the sacred fire.
Grandmothers and Grandfathers of the South,
We call you in for the emotional healing of her baby,
child, adult and elder,
Clearing those patterns that do not serve her.
Grandmothers and Grandfathers of the West,
We call you in for the healing of Marguerite's physical body
that does not serve her any more.
We ask for forgiveness of those who have harmed Marguerite.
Or those she might have harmed.
Grandfathers and Grandfathers of the North,
Bless her spirit and linage seven generations back

and call her Masters and guides for this transition.
Father Sky and Mother Earth,
We ask for a healing of her heart as she travels.
We ask for a healing of her third eye
and remove all sickness that might be in her spirit body.
We ask this in the name of all that is Holy.
We honor all people and religions.
Amen, Oh,"

"Thank you. I heard every word." Marquerite sighed through bleeding lips.

"Just as you are leaving your body tonight, I want you to go toward the Light. Don't look back. Don't look at the image of Laima or Lee. Do you understand? Don't look back. Let them go." Sally whistled and started to break up the vibration of fear she sensed around Marquerite's body. "If you look back, you'll be pulled into your body again. Do you hear me?!"

Wide-eyed, Marquerite nodded her head in agreement. She was ready for the magic roller coaster ride of her death. As she listened to Sally's toning, her whole body began to flutter. She was so thin. Her watermelon tumor tummy held her down like an anchor, as her arms flailed like a sail in a cross wind. A row of beaded sweat crowned her forehead. Pain locked her lips as she blew out air from her past.

"Don't take that pain with you, girl." It's as if Sally was in the room, calling out Satan during a Baptist Revival. "Let it go!"

Everyone in the room became uncomfortable with the shift in energy and Marquerite's tremendous effort. Sally was right. Looking back would keep Marquerite attached to us. She needed to go to her next life, to the souls waiting for her, to her God, to the Light.

I was so distraught; my body was rigid. Me, myself and I were numbed and tired. Sally started to guide her with color imagery, "Can you see a green light? I want you to wrap it around your tummy. Now wrap your whole body in Gold light. What is pulling you down into your body? Who do we need to forgive...?" It must have gone on for an hour; the questions, the heavy breathing, the sighing, the dying.

On the drive back to Lee's home, I remembered the quote from Seth, "You could not die unless you were the kind of creature who was born, nor could you have this present moment as you know it. Your body is aware of the fact of its death at birth and of its birth at its death, for all of its possibilities for action take place in the area between. Death is, therefore, as creative as birth and necessary for action and consciousness, in your terms."

Before falling asleep, my conversation with Joseph concerning Marquerite's passing echoed inside me, "Imagine me sitting on a white cloud, with mist coming down. The mist will become light that surrounds her. Now remember, when she passes over, find a key and lock a door. Stand in front of that door for about five minutes; then unlock the door and go through it. This past event will be sealed. By you doing this physically, it actualizes it in another realm. She will go soon."

The next morning will always be etched in my mind. Marguerite was not restless or nervous; she was frantic. She kept rearranging her Kleenex box, pencil and notebook pad, on the tray at her bedside. If Joseph were here, he would have done some sound work with her feeling of "dis-place-ment." Where was her placement?

Her eyes were pale with despair. Grabbing the pencil, she tried to write her name. The letters were so hard to form, which letter came first? I gently held her hand and smiled into her eyes, "You won't need this name any more." And we both began to cry. She fell asleep in my arms and I became mesmerized watching her chest rise and fall. "Ya' gonna fly real soon, love. Ya' gonna fly brave. You can do it." I whispered.

CHAPTER EIGHTEEN

"Quieting the Mind"

After Marquerite's death, there was a monkey on my back. I couldn't hold my focus. I had to keep going so I wouldn't remember and somehow I was always forgetting. I began to pray for a new teacher that could help me with this situation.

It came through six degrees of friendship.

Meditation came into my life, because a dear friend's brother taught transcendental meditation. Steven had gone through the certified course of instruction, my friend Linda and I became his students. Twenty minutes a day, we would practice transcendental meditation. Steven gave us a mantra that would help us focus our thoughts.

Only after meeting Joseph and later reading his book, Being in Vibration, did I begin to understand the impact of sound on the unconscious mind. Saying a mantra during the meditation helped me focus on a phrase. I wasn't disturbed by other thoughts, memories or sensations. Simply put the mantra replaced my thinking patterns. On a deeper level, saying the mantra vibrated throughout my body, having an effect on every cell. Most mantras have their value from the quality of the sound and its affect can be felt in the different vibration systems within one's body. In the beginning, I had a more basic need from meditation, besides quieting the mind. Sleep.

I was having problems remaining conscious; let alone perceiving the finer difference between "open attention" and "focused attention" needed for TM to work or saying a mantra and quieting the chatter. My body needed deep healing work. For the first six months of our practice, I would fall into a deep sleep; that relaxed my body and mind. I had the best doctor working on my body while I slept. It was my Higher Self and we hadn't been introduced yet.

Transcendental Meditation, or TM, as it was known in America, came from the Vedic traditions in India. It was introduced to thousands of people in 1958 and into the seventies, by Maharishi Mahesh Yogi.

America was ripe for something to quiet its collective mind. We had too much, too full, too everything. In India, this type of meditation was connected with the Hindi religion. In America, it became secular and was dubbed, "a practice for self-development."

In Bob Spitz's Biography of the Beatles, he wrote about them traveling to Rishikesh, India to study Transcendental Meditation at the feet of Maharishi Mahesh Yogi. From then on, meditation became the buzz word of the music world. With Maharishi's world tours, along with endorsements from celebrities who practiced it, TM became a house hold word. By 1980, over a million people were practitioners and I had gone from TM to Zen.

CHAPTER NINETEEN

"The Bear Society"

The letter stated, "On behalf of ZEN MOUNTAIN MONASTERY, I would like to thank you for joining our Board of Governors. Prajna Paraminta, John Daido Loori." I have always kept this letter, because it reminded me of an amazing man who had a passion for the arts and a very unique approach to teaching Zen. This comprehensive Zen program he created is detailed in his book, The Eight Gates of Zen.

At the young age of fourteen, John set up a darkroom in the family bathroom and started his passion for photography. Because of that love, he studied under the famous photographer Minor White and Minor White taught him to meditate. Finding Minor White was the first step toward becoming a Zen master and creating his amazing program. In 1980, John established the Zen Arts Center, at Mount Tremper, New York. Later it became the Zen Mountain Monastery.

When I met John, he was a Zen Master. In 1986, he was given dharma transmission by his teacher, Taizan Maezumi Roshi. It was a beautiful ceremony. What I remember most was the simple story he told me about having to give up his Hasselblad camera when he began his formal Zen practice. It made me clutch mine even harder.

I had gone to the monastery for a week's retreat which coupled meditation and photography. I wasn't interested in Zen Buddhism particularly. I did know meditation was good for my health and photography was my passion. What I came away with was a skewed sense of how to meditate and the experience of piercing the concept of two dimensional images. Each night, I clutched by Hasselblad tightly and put it under my pillow, remembering John's story.

In that week, I began to ever so slightly experience seeing this world differently. During my dream time, questions floated inside me: Who knew the way to be in the moment, capturing the essence on film so that it became the gateway into another dimension? Not I. Who knew the zafu, the legs crossed, the painful back, the wandering mind were all one? Not I. Who knew the pathway from seeing to being? Not I.

Only Beautiful Painted Arrow and studying some Buddhist scriptures were able to help me galvanize an understanding of our mind's ability to create images that were then put into physical form.

It would take a Rug Purrush, a 2,500-year lineage carrier, a Saint whose sole purpose was to teach the Vedic truths, a Swamiji of golden integrity, and a Guru with infinite patience to begin untying my karmic knots from the scarf of cosmic consciousness and teach me the deep process of meditation.

CHAPTER TWENTY

"The East West Bridge"

"Now Listen!" Sally Perry always knew when I was listening half-heartedly. "Are you there?" Our connection on the telephone was crystal clear, I wasn't.

"Yes, Yes." I felt like a school child being reprimanded. My Reiki practice was going well and who needed this long-distance event anyway. "Go ahead. When are you doing this?" The word "this" turned into a snarly hiss.

Her voice went up several notches, quivering with impatience. "The New Year's sweat lodge will be held at Sandbridge, Virginia. I want you there. It's o.k. if you do the lodge in your healing room, while we do ours in the physical form in Sandbridge. You will appear in spirit on the East Coast. In the West, you will be in physical form. Get ready. No food. You will be on a twenty-four hour fast before the lodge and you will be sitting in meditation while we do the lodge here. Do your prayers to the directions before you start your meditation."

The only sound I could make was, "Hmmm." This event demanded a stretching of consciousness, with as much awareness this brain could muster and store in my memory banks. The thought of all this focused work was making me grumpy. But she was my teacher and I was her student. I extended by commitment, "Hmmmmmmmm. How many prayer ties do you want me to do?"

"Do sixty-four in each direction. It will be a new beginning. A doorway into a new future for you."

"Hmmmmmmmm."

CHAPTER TWENTY-ONE
"The Lodge"

Both my mother and father knew and experienced the concept of a "sweat". In the Baltics, they were called saunas. My mother shared some of her stories of ceremonies done in the sauna. She enjoyed the story of "seeing" a newborn's future the most. When a child is born; the mother, grandmother, three women Elders and a Seer would go into a Sauna. The general translation of a clairvoyant from Estonian into English was a "seer". There inside the sauna, after water was poured on the heated rocks; the Seer would crack a goose egg and the contents of the egg would tell the future of the new born. In my father's homeland, Lithuania, a sweat bath or sauna was constructed of wood. Many ceremonies of healing were done in the sauna.

I grew up in the United States and so the tradition of my ancestors would come through the Elders that came to me here in America. My three teachers for the American Sweat lodge were: Joseph Rael, Beautiful Painted Arrow of Southern Ute and Picuris Pueblo descent; Fred Wahpepah, Kickapoo-Sac and Fox Elder, and Sally Perry, whose grandmother on her father's side was from the Cherokee Nation.

There are many forms of sweat lodges. Under the guidance of these teachers the lodge was made by placing blankets on a dome made of willow branches. Lodge stones were heated in a fire outside the lodge. Then they were carried into the lodge and the lodge door was covered with blankets. Sometimes herbs or oils were placed upon stones. The stones were blessed and placed into a hole in the center of the lodge. The Lodge Leader would pour water over the rocks and the prayers began. When the sweat was finished, the participants would leave the lodge to participate in a feast of thanksgiving.

My greatest perspective about this ceremony was given to me when I first came to California. While living in Ojai, my friend J.J. and I opened our land to ceremony, so that a lodge might be built there. Words flew like some invisible smoke signals that a lodge graced the Ojai valley, different nations came. Each Nation having their ways with specific colors for directions, who poured the water, proper clothing, men's lodge, women's lodge, ceremonies for the dead, and healing for the living.

One early Saturday morning, a gang of twenty-one bikers drove up, parked and put their guns on the kitchen table. By 10 a.m., their Elder arrived in a red 1968 El Dorado Cadillac. All the men followed the directions of their Elder and the lodge was quickly covered with blankets and the fire started. They had their sweat, shared fried bread and smoked meat. As they left, one muscular Indian, wearing a Harley t-shirt, leaned over his bike with a bowed head and whispered, "If there is anything you need, ma'am, just call. We will be here. Thank you again."

I smiled. I never had a brother. It was my first sense of family protection in America. For J.J., it was the first time she nearly fainted.

What I began to see was the universal element Mother Earth. Once the Elder spoke to start the ceremony, everything was sacred, everybody became aligned with the Mother and the Father. All were in gratitude. There was no right or wrong way, only the red road.

At this time, during this specific lodge in Sandbridge, Sally was asking me to do something with time and shape shifting. She was asking me to focus on two realms over an extended period of time; to be present in physical form in Davis and aware of the sweat ceremony in Sandbridge. The blackness of my healing room would become a screen of awareness and my sweatlodge. I had read the work of Thomas Mails and his dialogue with the great Sioux Holy Man, Fools Crow. Fools Crow wrapped himself in a medicine blanket to shut out the world and used the darkness as a screen to obtain information about the illness of his patient. Several times in the darkness of the lodge, I would see images of constellations and images of people. After the lodge, I asked Joseph what they meant. He would place his right hand on my shoulder, smile and say, "Good." Then with a quick turn, walk away and start a conversation with another person. Many years later, Joseph shared some of his childhood experiences in the Kiva with me and how the walls opened up for him. Sally wanted me to be in Davis and in Sandbridge. The blackness of my room would become a screen for me to project into the Sandbridge lodge.

Learning to stretch consciousness paper thin with total awareness would be a life-long, developing skill, over many life times.

With no food, a whole bunch of prayer ties to be made; before New Year's Eve, I was a grumpy bear. Here was the formula: put one Baltic bear with an attitude inside a small room with no light. Total darkness. Black. No sense of placement or expansion and painful physical discomfort of sitting for many hours. That is what I experienced for the most part: physical discomfort and a deep blackness during my meditation. My head felt like it was going to split open and often to keep the pain at bay, I would focus my eyes on my hands that seemed to be emanating white light. Nothing extraordinary, except for him.

CHAPTER TWENTY-TWO

"Following the Dream"

"How was it?" That's how Sally started our conversation when she called after the lodge.

"How was it?" I screamed in my head. That was the way you ask someone who just went grocery shopping on a Friday night before a major rock concert on the weekend. "How was it!" You forgot your shopping list at home; the woman in front of you had a breakdown because her credit card was not accepted, and they ran out of hot dogs! How can Walmart run out of hot dogs on this weekend? I should have gone to Safeway, but you can't park there! "How was it?" The chatter went running up and down the shopping aisles of my head.

"It went well." I said in a very quiet voice, timid as a church mouse. Totally detached from my emotions, I understood nothing. My body hurt, only the vision of a man in orange stood out in my memory bank. The man with the frizzy hair. Nobody wears orange and exaggerated frizzy hair. I shook my head to feel my hair, could it ever get that frizzy? Who was he and didn't he appear in Woodstock?

"It went well." I took in a deep breath. "There was this man, that appeared."

Now it was Sally's turn, "Hummmmmm. Did I tell you what I did in the summer of 95'? It has something to do with you now."

Yes or no, I was going to hear her story.

"You see." She started out, "I always." She drew out the word "always" the way every Southern lady would. "I always follow instructions from my guides." Her Southern accent started a cadence that fully captivated me;

"I was going to give a reading in Georgia. I loved driving alone. Singing and listening to Elvis, it was a joy to be alive. Well, somehow I got lost after four hours of driving. I ask my guides for help and they gave me explicit instructions. "Turn left at the next stop sign, it's a dirt road. Drive three miles. Make another left turn. It was dusty as hell and I had to roll up the windows. Make a right turn. I knew I was lost somehow. But I kept following my guides. Finally, through the dust, a small town appeared: grocery store, post office and a gas station. I pulled under the awning of the gas station. Off to the left side, at the entrance of the auto shop were three young, strapping good looking men. They were huddled over a Ford Pickup truck. Kind of a rusty brown color, I think. I rolled down the window and waved for help. They paid me no mind. Then I waved and yelled. Desperation was beginning to creep into my words. The heat can do that to you. It was as if they were transfixed over something under the hood. Well, I was hot, lost and no one was listening. So, I got out of the car with my map in hand and banged the car door shut. The sound of the car door slamming broke their trance and the three looked up to see me for the first time. I waved them over and they reluctantly sauntered toward my car. "I'm lost and need help," I said.

Just as the three huddled around me, a huge pop filled the air, then smoke and fire erupted out of the truck engine. Had they been there, their faces, hands, God knows what would have been burned off. Instead the timing was right for intervention. That event forever taught me to follow my guides without question, no matter how crazy it all seemed."

Most of us are blind and deaf to the awareness of our guides, let alone our ancestors. But She Who Dances, Ms. Sally Perry, had been listening from a young age. Three young men's lives were saved because Sally Perry listened to her guides and at that moment, I was trying to remember and listen.

"What did he look like?" Sally seemed to be using her words carefully as she listened to me describe the man who kept appearing in my make-shift-lodge-meditation room. "Hmmmmmmm." I closed my eyes to see better and hummed again, "Hmmmmmmm. He was tall, big, kind of a flat nose, wearing an orange robe. His left hand was extended, palm up as if holding something. He had black, bushy, curly hair."

"Sai Baba? Satya Sai Baba. The reincarnation of Sai Baba of Shirdi. That's who it was. No doubt about it. That reminds me about my dear friend, Jeanne and how she was supposed to see Sai Baba. Go to his Ashram in India. You remember Alex? Alex Orbito, the psychic surgeon from the Philippines had done psychic surgery on her and removed a tumor from her breast. It was Alex that told her she needed to see Sai Baba. He would have to pull out the roots of her karma, in order for his healing to be complete. Yes, I remember all of it." Sally took in a huge breath and started talking again. "I had my first vision of Sai Baba two years earlier; I was doing a healing on Jeanne. Sai Baba always wore orange. I remember now he had instructed Jeanne to go to India and see him. We were both awestruck that the reincarnation of Sai Baba of Shirdi graced us with his vision and instruction. Now, here he comes to you with an outstretched hand. Hmmmmmmmm, Ha!" she breathed out.

Her "Hmmmmm," was beginning to sound like a train whistle in my ear and her voice seemed to get louder. My feelings were becoming prickly. Something was coming, fast as a freight train. Nothing could stop it. The feelings of a caged animal crept into my psyche. Just like the first time I met Joseph, my whole body became agitated. I couldn't sit still. I got up and started to pace, pressing the phone receiver into my ear until it hurt. The caged cat inside me wanted to bolt. Drop the receiver, Druskis. Run as fast as you can, before the train hits you. My heart was pounding. Then she said it and all I heard was "India."

The next moment, her voice became muted, as if she were yelling down a long, dark shaft. The words were muffled. "I'm taking a group to India, to Sai Baba's cave. I want you to be part of that."

"Which part?" I was grasping for some sense of reality; my body was sweating. I never wanted to go to India. The Baltics, ride The Oriental Express, Mongolia, but not India.

"Start meditating. You must read, Autobiography of a Yogi. Let's see, I did enjoy, Living with the Himalayan Masters by Swami what's his name? Yes, it was Swami Rama. Maybe Janet can help you with booking your flight. You'll need a visa."

"A visa card?" I whispered, wanting to cry.

"No silly girl. A visa to get into the country." Her voice was light and strong at the same time. "Oh, dear. I have another call coming in. Let me get back to you."

I didn't have to go, I had to go. The ocean current of my destiny was pulling me under. Not even the life boat of "why" could save me now.

THE END

REFERENCE READING

Chapter One ~ Joseph
Utes – The Mountain People by Jan Pettit
Tracks of Dancing Light by Joseph E. Rael and Lindsay Sutton

Chapter Two ~ Dreaming of the Future in Present Time
Being & Vibration by Joseph Rael with Mary Elizabeth Marlow
Ceremonies of the Living Spirit by Joseph Rael

Chapter Three ~ The First Dance Is the Best Dance
Chronicles of A Healer, She Who Dances by Sally Perry
Embracing the Healing Mind by Sally Perry Brown
The Art of Dreaming by Carlos Castaneda

Chapter Four ~ The First Day
The Power of Silence by Carlos Castaneda

Chapter Five ~ After One Comes Two
The Wonderful Life and Teachings of Shri Baba by Shri Sai Satcharita
Shri Sai Baba by Swami Sai Sharan Anand / translated by V.B. Kher
Sai Baba, Man of Miracles by Howard Murphet

Chapter Six ~ Opening the Western Gate
The Sacred Pipe, Black Elk's Account of the Seven Rites of the Oglala Sioux
Recorded & Edited by Joseph Epes Brown
Cosmic Crystals, Crystal Consciousness of the New Age by Ra Bonewitz
A How-to Pamphlet on Walking by Beautiful Painted Arrow

Chapter Seven ~ Know the Wave, Be the Ocean
Love is in the Earth, A Kaleidoscope of Crystals Updated by Melody
The Crystal Connection, A Guidebook for Personal and Planetary Ascension
by Randall N. Baer and Vicki Baer

REFERENCE READING

Chapter Eight ~ Kiva Journal
Conversations with Sathya Sai Baba by John Hislop
The Visionary, Entering the Mystic Universe of Joseph Rael Beautiful Painted Arrow by Kurt Wilt, PhD and forward by Joseph Rael
Keys of Enoch by J.J. Hurtak

Chapter Nine ~ Finding One's Self
The Sacred Paw, The Bear, in Nature, Myth and Literature
by Paul Shepard and Barry Sanders
The Grizzly Bear, The Narrative of a Hunter-Naturalist
by William H. Wright
The Ghost Dance, An Untold History of the Americas
by Michel Stuart Ani
Sun-Moon Dancing: Medicine for our Time
by Rick Cotroneo, Dancing Light

Chapter Ten ~ Fly Brave

Chapter Eleven ~ Healing House
Spiritual Intelligence, What We Can Learn from the Early Awakening Child
by Marsha Sinetar
The Nature of The Psyche, Its Human Expression (A Seth Book)
by Jane Roberts
Empowerment Through Reiki, the Path to Personal and Global Transformation by Paula Horan
Your Body Doesn't Lie by John Diamond, M.D.
Esoteric Anatomy, The Body as Consciousness by Bruce Burger
Fusion of the Five Elements One by Mantak Chia and Manewan Chia
Awaken Healing Light of the Tao by Mantak and Maneewan Chia
Pranic Psychotherapy by Choa Kok Sui
Healing Memories in Seconds by Gary Sinclair

REFERENCE READING

Chapter Twelve ~ The Flower of Life
The Hidden You, A Journey Into the Human Energy System: The Chakras by Walter Makichen
Australian Bush Flower Essences by Ian White
Bush Flower Healing by Ian White
Australian Bush Flower Remedies by Ian White
The Ancient Secret of the Flower of Life, Volume 2 by Drunvalo Melchizedek

Chapter Thirteen ~ Living the Vision
Mandukya Upnishad, True Method of Self-Realization
by Achrya Mahamandaleshwar Yugpurush Swami Parmanand

Chapter Fourteen ~ Knowing Your Truth
The Hidden You, A Journey Into the Human Energy System: The Chakras by Walter Makichen
Jesus, The Son of Man by Kahlil Gibran

Chapter Fifteen ~ Both Are Healed
Thinking in Pictures by Temple Grandin
Back to A Future For Mankind by Ibrahim Karim, Ph.D, Dr. Sc.
Aurajin, Recognizing Spirit in Matter by Carol Klesow

Chapter Sixteen ~ Seven Times Seven
Divine Posture Influence upon Endocrine Glands by Cajzoran Ali

Chapter Seventeen ~ The Art of Dying
Nature Spirits & Elemental Beings, Working with the Intelligence in Nature by Marko Pogacnik
Coma: The Dreambody Near Death by Arnold Mindell
Facing Death and Finding Hope by Christine Longaker

Chapter Eighteen ~ Quieting the Mind
The Mind Rules by John A. Zulli

REFERENCE READING

The Brain That Changes Itself by Norman Doidge, M.D.

Chapter Nineteen ~ The Bear Society
Letters to Aspirants by Clara M. Codd
Estonian Story of a Nation by "Editors"
Lithuania Through the Ages by Dr. A. Sapoka

Chapter Twenty ~ East West Bridge
Autobiography of a Yogi by Paramahansa Yogananda
Life and Teaching of Sri Anandamayi Ma by Dr. Alexander Lpski

Chapter Twenty-One ~ The Lodge
Native American Architecture by Peter Nabokov and Robert Easton
The Heart Sutra, Becoming a Buddha through Meditation by Osho

Chapter Twenty-Two ~ Following the Dream
Born to Heal by Jaime T. Licauco
Faith Healing and Psychic Surgery by Jesus B. Lava, M.D. and Antonio S. Araneta, D. Phil
Living with Himalayan Masters by Swami Rama
Body Consciousness to Soul Consciousness
by Mahamandaleshawar Yug Purush Swami Parmanand Giri Maharaj Ji

ABOUT THE AUTHOR

At the age of seven, Laima took up the camera wanting to share her vision of this amazing complex world. Laima has spent most of her artistic photography career in Manhattan. She has shown with Andy Warhol and other artists in New York City. She has been published in major magazines and her commercial clients include: Chase Banking, Lincoln Center, Prentice Hall Publishing.

With a rich family background in healing, Laima has been a meditation teacher and a Reiki Master for 10 years. Her lineage of Reiki teachers has a direct line to Dr. Mikaomi Usui, who discovered the Reiki healing technique in Japan. When she had her healing practice in Davis, California, her goal was to teach techniques that allowed every client to develop their innate skills for their highest potential.

In the past fifteen years, Laima has been documenting positive images of Autistic adults, and after obtaining her special education certificate, enjoys teaching these very special people.

For more information visit:
www.LaimaDruskis.com

Made in the USA
Las Vegas, NV
11 January 2022

41043038R10135